To Debbie
With love from
Bryan

MY SMALL SHARE

A Quaker Diary from WWI

Ernest W. Pettifer

Edited with a Memoir by
Bryan G.E. Pettifer

authorHOUSE®

AuthorHouse™ UK Ltd.
1663 Liberty Drive
Bloomington, IN 47403 USA
www.authorhouse.co.uk
Phone: 0800.197.4150

Published by AuthorHouse   05/22/2014

ISBN: 978-1-4969-7903-2 (sc)
ISBN: 978-1-4969-7905-6 (hc)
ISBN: 978-1-4969-7904-9 (e)

Library of Congress Control Number: 2014907903

Contents

Memoir of Ernest W. Pettifer

The Man who Volunteered for the Friends
    Ambulance Unit in 1915 ix
The Friends Ambulance Unit (F.A.U.) xi
Queen Alexandra Hospital, Dunkirk xiv
Postscript—After the War xvi
Acknowledgements xvii
Contemporary Map xviii

The Diary

1. Dunkirk and the Queen Alexandra Hospital 3
    February 3-April 21, 1917

2. A Visit to the Front 16
    April 23, 1917

3. In the Midst of War Life Goes on 21
    April 25-June 11, 1917

4. Attacked from Air, Land and Sea 30
    September 6-October 31, 1917

5. A Month of Incessant Bombardment. 38
    September 6-October 31, 1917

6. A Quieter Spell but only Comparatively! 56
    November 1-December 27, 1917

7. The Air War 63
    January 5-February 17, 1918

8. Moving the Hospital while still under Fire 70
    February 18-March 26, 1918

9. Fears for Dunkirk as a German Offensive Threatens 77
    March 27-May 15, 1918

10. A Long Summer of Stalemate 82
    June 5-September 27, 1918

11. The Final Push 95
    September 28-November 1, 1918

12. Visit to Bruges and the Move to Courtrai. 98
    November 2-3, 1918

13. The Great Shadow Lifted 104
    November 4-December 31 1918

14. So Ends My War 112
    January 1-February 7, 1919

Appendix—War Medals 117

Memoir of
Ernest W. Pettifer
by his son
Bryan G.E. Pettifer

**Ernest W. Pettifer in the uniform of the
Friends Ambulance Unit**

The Man who Volunteered
for the Friends Ambulance Unit
in 1915

Ernest Pettifer was born in 1882 and grew up in Newbury. He had a strict protestant upbringing in the closing years of the reign of Queen Victoria. He was a sporty character who would gather his friends together to form a football team and arrange matches with other teams.

This was the golden age of pedal cycling before the arrival in any numbers of the motor car and he wrote in later life of the "lovely countryside of South Berkshire and North Hampshire", which he had explored with great delight by bicycle and on foot. At the time of the War Ernest was still a bachelor and Newbury remained the family home, which he departed from, and returned to, while serving abroad.

Ernest was widely read, completing all of Dicken's books during his childhood. In preparation for his first book, *Punishments of Former Days,* he not only read previous authorities on the subject and general histories but reflected on and quoted from much wider literature. "Among the novelists and other writers, Scott, Dickens, Sir Walter Besant, Rafael Sabatini, Sir Arthur Conan Doyle, H.V. Morton and many others furnish vivid illustrations of the application of former methods of trial and punishment . . ." His wide reading provided a literary resource, which is evident in the diary and in the extensive range of his subsequent publications.

Ernest's Father was Magistrates' Clerk in Newbury and he and his two brothers followed their Father and became his assistants in the Newbury court. Ernest moved from Newbury to Wellington and then to Doncaster in about 1904 as an assistant, becoming the Clerk of the Doncaster West Riding Magistrates in 1913. The Court's work expanded as new coal mining pits were sunk around Doncaster in the early decades of the century, increasing enormously the population of the area.

When Ernest moved to Doncaster, he joined the Adult School Movement, an organisation founded by the Society of Friends or Quakers. As a result of his participation in it, Ernest was drawn into the Society of Friends and became a member of the Doncaster Meeting.

The FAU training camp at Jordans

Ambulance Train XI (Ernest seated at left)

The Friends Ambulance Unit
(F.A.U.)

The Society of Friends was predominantly pacifist but early in the war formed the Friends Ambulance Unit, which initially engaged in relief work with refugees. As the war developed it cared for the wounded in a number ways. It staffed casualty clearing stations near the front line, known by the French whom they served as Sections Sanitaire Anglaise (S.S.A.) They used motorised ambulances to ferry casualties from the front line. Other volunteers worked on ambulance trains evacuating casualties from the forward areas. Others staffed civilian and military hospitals.

Ernest volunteered to join the Friends Ambulance Unit in November 1915. He went to the newly set up FAU training camp at Jordans in Buckinghamshire.

He joined the staff of Ambulance Train X1 on January 26 1916 at Sotteville on the edge of Rouen. The train was composed of 21 assorted French wagons and coaches, only four of which were connected by corridors. When the train was on the move, communication with the non-corridor coaches had to be made during casual stops or by agile climbing along the footboards outside the train and hanging on to the door handles! In the winter there was no heating in the carriages except that generated in the kitchen.

In May the train was evacuating casualties from the first battle of Vimy Ridge and in July from the great battle of the Somme. During those battles the demand was very intense, trains needing to carry as many as double the normal complement and on one occasion three trips were made to the front in 48 hours. By August 18, 6,000 patients had been moved.

The Third Report of the FAU published in "The Friend" in November 1916 lists him as working in the King George Hospital in London. He is described as Quarter Master Sergeant and he has the oversight of over 100 members of the FAU who were working in the hospital as orderlies.

**A doctor moving from carriage to carriage on
the footboard of a train while in motion.**

Queen Alexandra Hospital, Malo les Bains

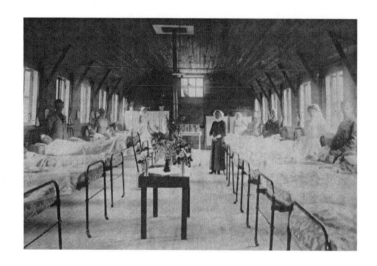

"A" ward at the Queen Alexandra Hospital

Queen Alexandra Hospital, Dunkirk

After a period of leave in late January 1917, Ernest sailed back to France to work in the Queen Alexandra Hospital in Malo-les-Bains, a district of Dunkirk, which is the principal setting for the diary. The Hospital had been created in the early months of 1915 to cope with British and French casualties and it grew to become one of the largest of the military hospitals until it finally closed to patients in December 1918.

Dunkirk has ancient earthwork fortifications with a grassy bank, the *glacis* referred to several times in the text of the diary, which ran from the fortifications down to the moat. The land selected for the Hospital was close by and less than half a mile from the sea front. The site was very vulnerable to bombing and shelling from sea and land. In consequence it was decided early in 1918 to move the Hospital to a new site in the grounds of the Chateau de Petite Synthe, about a mile and a half to the south west of Dunkirk.

Ernest was initially listed as one of four clerks working in the administration of the Hospital. This did not preclude direct involvement with patients. The diary frequently refers to the hurried removal of patients from the wards to the dugouts when the sirens sounded. He seems to have had a special responsibility for some of the most dangerously disturbed and shell-shocked patients.

In December 1917 he was appointed Administrative Superintendent of the Hospital, including managing all hospital personnel and responsibility for the grounds and for constructing new dugouts when needed. Labour forces of Chinese and other nationalities were employed in major construction work of this kind.

In February and March, 1918 he was responsible for the preparation of the new site for the hospital at the Chateau de Petite Synthe. After a shell had fallen in the old Hospital in the middle of the night of March 24, 1918, all the patients and staff and a considerable amount of stores were moved to the new site in the course of two hours, a remarkable achievement.

In November 1918 Ernest is moved to the civilian hospital at the Ambulance du Fort in Courtrai, in formerly enemy occupied territory where he stays until early February 1919.

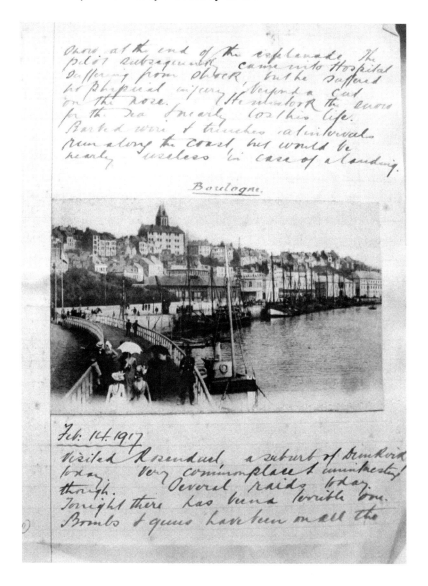

A sample page from the handwritten diary

Postscript—After the War

Initially Ernest wrote his diary in two small pocket books. After the war he wrote it as the diary presented here, illustrating it with postcards, photos (some of which are no longer reproducible) and newspaper cuttings collected at the time. There are spells, sometimes of a week or two when the diary records that nothing of great interest was happening. The diary has been edited to remove entries of limited interest and to highlight the major phases of the work. To give more of a sense of the movement of the events, the diary has been divided into chapters with headings and brief summaries.

Ernest returned to his post as Magistrates' Clerk early in 1919. Very sadly his brother Reginald, who had deputised for him during the war, developed pneumonia and died on December 2nd 1921. In 1926 Ernest married Hilda Muriel Turner and they had three children, Joyce, Bryan and Lorna. In the closing years of his life he was able to know his first grandchild, Alasdair. As he fed him in his highchair on one occasion he recalled the experience of feeding patients in the hospital.

I recall that when I was 8 years old he joined us as we were getting ready for bed, which was unusual. His anxiety was palpabable and was evident even to me as a child. British forces had just been evacuated from Dunkirk and the country felt that a German invasions, for which we were ill prepared, would soon follow. Ernest may well have been recalling also the anxiety, which the diary recounts, that Dunkirk would be cut off by the German Spring offensive in 1918.

He published three books, *Punishments of Former Days* (1939), *The Court is Sitting* (1940) and *The Court Resumes* (1945). He wrote a number of articles for the *Justice of the Peace* and in retirement he had a regular column in *The Doncaster Chronicle*.

He was President of the Magistrates' Clerks Society, 1947-1948. In 1954 he was awarded the degree of Master of Arts by the University of Sheffield. He retired in 1958 after completing 45 years as Magistrates' Clerk and died just short of his 80th birthday on the 3rd March 1962.

Acknowledgements

I would like to thank all who assisted in the production of this diary. Norma Jones typed it from the handwritten manuscript. Mike Stone, Barbara Large and Geoff Fisher gave helpful advice. Melissa Atkinson of the Library at the Religious Society of Friends and Rosemary Bavister of Taylor and Francis Books (UK) assisted in the search for copyright of the illustrations.

A number of illustrations have been taken from *The Friends Ambulance Unit 1914-1919* edited by M. Tatham and J.E. Miles. Ernest Proctor's charcoal drawings vividly illustrate both the handwritten diary and the official history of the FAU. It is understood that he died in 1935.

Every effort has been made to trace and contact copyright holders. If there are any inadvertent omissions we apologise to those concerned, and ask that you contact the publishers so that we can correct any oversight as soon as possible.

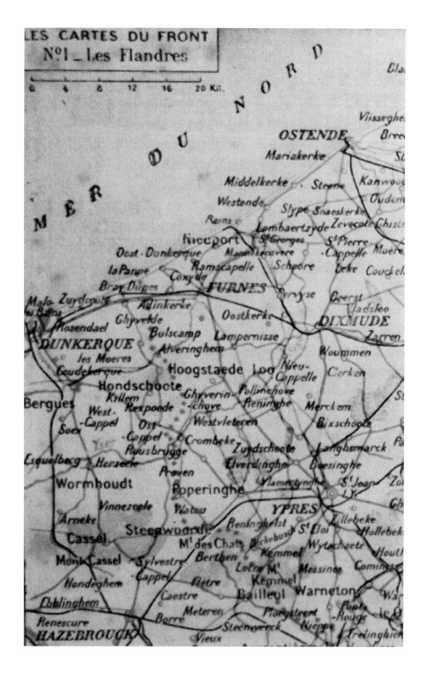

West section of a contemporary map included in the diary

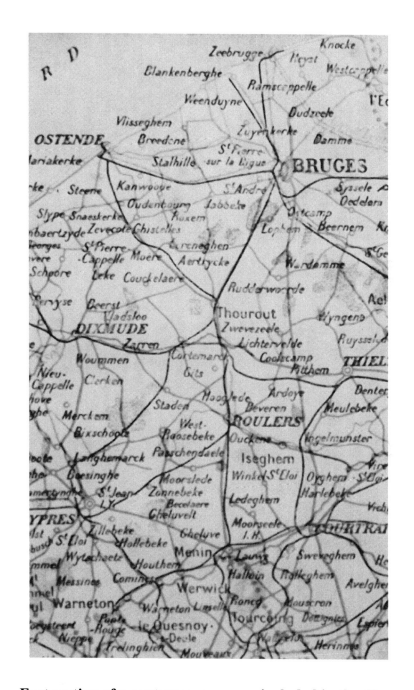

East section of a contemporary map included in the diary

The War Diary of Ernest W. Pettifer

February 3, 1917 To February 7, 1919

1

DUNKIRK AND THE QUEEN ALEXANDRA HOSPITAL

Ernest had crossed to France before when he was working on Ambulance Trains XI but this time the sighting of mines in the English Channel results in delays. As he explores the Dunkirk area we have glimpses of his keen interest in the natural world especially the bird life.

February 3, 1917

I left Newbury by the 8.40 am train and after calling at HQ caught the 12.50 pm boat train from Charing Cross. C.H. Bird and J.Z. Smith went down with me, both going out for the first time. Very wintry weather and Kent was under snow. There was a big crowd of soldiers for the boat, and after the usual formalities we got on board to find things pretty congested. After waiting an hour everyone had to disembark, the sailing being cancelled owing to mines in the straits.

We were billeted at 6 West Avenue, Folkestone (Mrs Wolf) for the night and had quite decent quarters. We had a walk along the Leas and later towards East Cliff but it was fearfully slippery and very cold. Clear moonlit night though the sea looked splendid.

February 4, 1917

Boat again cancelled. More snow in the night. We walked along the Leas as far as Sandgate Castle in the morning and got back to find message awaiting us that boat would sail at 2.00 pm but were again sent back. After dinner we went to Hythe by motorbus and visited St Leonards Church and its famous crypt. There are bones here of 4,000 persons. We walked back along the sea wall through Seabrook and Sandgate. Rapid thaw set in and streets became very slushy. Two kinds of gulls are very common (probably herring gulls and lesser black-headed gull.) An airship was patrolling the straits and several destroyers were visible.

February 5, 1917

Fresh snow in the night and it was horribly bleak. We got on the boat about 9.30 am and sailed at 10.30 am (S.S. Onward) Sun shining at start but we ran into snow storms halfway out. Several destroyers and a large flight of gulls acted as escorts. Saw V-shaped flight or string of ducks proceeding rapidly towards France and several small birds. "Western Australia" (one of four hospital ships) was in Boulogne Harbour.

SS Onward sailing from Boulogne harbour

Had lunch at Hotel de France and walked round city walls in the afternoon. Snow very deep here. Left at 5.00 pm to catch train for Calais. Station not heated and very slushy and dirty. Waited 5 ¼ hours. Wickedly cold. Train came at 10.00 pm and we crawled to Calais. Never had such a journey. Windows, floor and ourselves frozen. Got to Calais at 2.00 am to find connecting train gone.

Station very miserable; no fire and no food. Alternately thawed and froze at a brazier outside, until it got too bad so three soldiers and I set off to find some food and warmth. Dreary prowl through silent streets until another chap and I stumbled across a French soldier's shelter where we got some coffee and a penny roll. Great stuff to us though and we warmed at stove for an hour. Had rattling good breakfast at Hotel Sauvage at 7.30 am and washed and shaved and felt better. Only 2fr 50c.

Calais, lighthouse and tram

Calais, town square and belfry

Walked round Calais with one of South Staffords. I saw old and new lighthouses, several armed trawlers going out, monument to the 7 Burghers (1347) and another to the fallen French in various wars. This is a custom at most French towns and a pleasing one. Barges all frozen in and the wind was piercingly cold. Lunch at Sauvage (1fr 50c): very good and cheap. I saw a man with a number of dead sparrows on a string, presumably on sale for food.

Left 1.25 pm. Country to Dunkirk very flat. Rooks and grey crows in fields. Sedgy grasses in every ditch, all leaning towards the West. Snow very deep everywhere.

Reported at Hotel Pyl on arrival, a big and busy place. Found many men there I knew formerly at King George Hospital or on Ambulance Train XI. Detailed to Queen Alexandra Hospital where there were other men I knew.

February 7, 1917

The hospital is of wood and plaster and seems well equipped. It is altogether in the hands of the unit and patients are half English and half French, the latter having always to be guaranteed 80 beds. Walked along jetty but wind and snow were too much and I had to turn back. Anti-aircraft station, cold job for the poor beggars there these nights and they have to be well awake too. By the way three raids last night for fourth successive night. Call for ambulance for two women hit by bomb tonight.

February 8, 1917

Still bitterly cold. Everything frozen in bedroom. An air raid as we were getting up.

I walked along the jetty and the docks in the evening. I saw two monitors, very interesting vessels and the first I had seen. *[Monitors— shallow draft, heavily armoured, shore bombardment vessels.]* The size of the docks surprised me. It is said to be the third biggest port in France. On a cafe facing the prison is this original sign: "On est bien mieux ici qu'en face" (It is better to be here than at the front.")

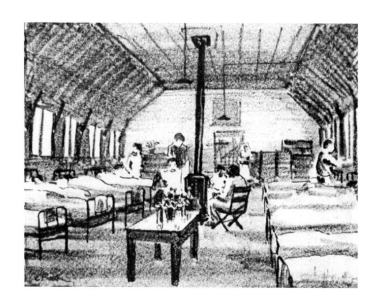

A ward in the Queen Alexandra Hospital

The central court of the hospital
(E. Proctor)

The Cathedral has been badly knocked about in the raids and bombardments, one side being absolutely roofless. The Town Hall is a fine brick and stone building.

At 9.00 pm there was another heavy raid and fierce firing from the ships and batteries. Three soldiers were brought here. One died on admission (throat veins severed), a second had right leg shattered and a third was hit in thigh slightly. Flaming darts were used by anti-aircraft guns, having the appearance of rockets before bursting; a long trail of fire. I have a wretched cold, result of journey from Boulogne, I suppose.

February 9, 1917

Day opened with further raid by four taubes. *[Taube (German for dove or pigeon)—German monoplane, used in the early part of the war for bombing and surveillance.]* I saw one and others saw three. Heavy firing, spraying the district with shrapnel, without result as usual. Wounded man brought in as a result of the raid (shrapnel in neck.) Bombs last night very close to us, one at Malo Church.

Dunkirk Lighthouse

78 DUNKERQUE. — La Cale des Pêcheurs — LL

Dunkirk Fishing Port

February 11, 1917

A thaw at last, thank goodness! The guns at the front can be heard today, just over 20 miles away. Went to English Church at 6.30 pm with Adams and Peile. Church lit by candles stuck on outer edges of seat. No choir. Very helpful and reverent service. All soldiers, save a few nurses, present.

February 12, 1917

Went over to "Cat and Fiddle", Recreation Hut at docks, run by Unit, very successfully on lines of YMCA huts. Monitor, "General Wolfe" in dock, a fine ship, and several armed auxiliaries. The docks are very fine and far exceeded my expectations.

Shelters for air raids are indicated by notices in red on the doors of houses. Sirens and a hooter, popularly known as "The Cow", because of its resemblance to the sounds emitted by that useful animal, give warning of raids, generally after the raid is over!! No raid today. Weather damp and misty with rivers of slush everywhere.

February 13, 1917

An overturned seaplane lay on the snow at the end of the esplanade. The pilot subsequently came into hospital suffering from shock, but he suffered no physical injury, beyond a cut on the nose. He mistook the snow for the sea and nearly lost his life. Barbed wire and trenches at intervals run along the coast, but would be nearly useless in the event of a landing.

Cat and Fiddle Recreation Hut at the Docks

February 14, 1917

Visited Rosendael, a suburb of Dunkirk today. Very common place and uninteresting though. Several raids today. Tonight there has been a terrible one. Bombs and guns have been on all the evening.

The sky was alive with shrapnel at 5.30 p.m. and three hostile machines were visible. A workshop at the R.N.A.S. aerodrome was destroyed by a bomb. Two men were killed and 15 injured, and some of the latter are not likely to recover. It has been a busy night in Hospital and ordinary patients have had to turn out of bed to make room for wounded. The Germans seem to know Dunkirk very accurately. They fly at a great height and always come in from the sea.

February 15, 1917

Nineteen patients altogether from the last raid, two of whom died soon after admission and one this morning. At night I went to the beach. Star shells were bursting over the sea and the monitors were firing frantically, but at what I do not know.

February 16, 1917

Raid at 7.00 am. Three taubes visible. Heavy firing and one piece of shell hit the roof of our barrack room. Hooded crows are very common on the sands, probably attracted by the flotsam and jetsam washed up. A meat ship was torpedoed outside recently and a lot of the carcasses of meat have been washed up.

February 20, 1917

The dunes are a wilderness of sandhills and pools in winter and are very depressing and monotonous. I have been reading Stevenson's "Catriona" and am interested to find that it refers to the sand dunes of Dunkirk.

March 8, 1917

One of the French patients attacked a Sister with a razor and cut her neck and throat. A V.A.D. pluckily took the razor from him or she probably would have been killed. He apparently had some grievance against her and I do not think she is free from blame. We heard today that "Glenart Castle" (F.A.U. Hospital ship) had been mined.

Hospital Ship "Glenart Castle." Facing p. 194

**Friends Ambulance Unit Hospital Ship
Glenart Castle**

11

36. - Environs de DUNKERQUE. - Le Sanatorium de Zuydcoote (Côté Nord)

The French Military Hospital at Zuydcoote

March 11, 1917

I walked out to Zuydcoote where there is a huge sanatorium, now a military hospital.

March 15, 1917

A Royal Berks. man brought in late, dead, skull crushed by falling timber at docks. Also body of man drowned eight weeks ago.

March 17, 1917

Raids started again. One dropped 100 yards away and hit three of our drivers and smashed every window of nurses quarters.

Sister injured by French patient received Croix de Guerre from General Boision.

March 18, 1917

Walked beyond St Pol, on the coast. Larks were singing and we found some daisies in flower, wild ducks, crested larks, grey crows and gulls.

H.M. minesweeper "Duchess of Montrose" struck a mine outside Dunkirk and sank in two minutes. Twenty men missing, two killed and eight in hospital. Three were brought here, a lieutenant and two ratings. One of latter said she was blown to bits. He was in water 15 minutes, clinging to piece of wood, unable to swim a stroke.

March 24, 1917

Went to a concert at Pyl by a hospital party. In the middle the guns started firing heavily and nearly all lights had to go out. Many bombs were dropped. Later five men were brought to hospital, one was already dead, hit in the face as he stood at the door of the dugout. All were Royal Berks. men again. Their camp always seems to suffer. Another man was hit at the docks.

March 25, 1917

Naval raid during the night and terrific row from the guns. The sky was lit up by flashes and the scream of the shells could be distinctly heard overhead. Several pieces of shell fell on the hospital.

March 26, 1917

One soldier brought in today, dead, killed by shell. It is difficult to get accurate news of raid, but the real damage seems to have been small, although I have never heard heavier shelling. I had to take in a dead man, a horrible sight; killed as he lay on his bed, poor fellow, while his comrades on either side were unhurt.

March 30, 1917

We had a very horrible raid tonight, starting about 9.00 pm and continuing about an hour and a half. Many bombs were dropped and the gunfire was tremendous. I hear it is stated that 2,000 shells were fired. The hostile planes flew very low and could be heard distinctly. Several times they used their machine guns to fire at the batteries, firing down the search light beams. Shrapnel, bullets and fragments of shell fell in showers all around us and on the Hospital, several bombs dropped within a hundred yards. The patients were very terrified and we had to sit with some, while many of those who could get to the dugout refused to come out.

March 31, 1917

Considering the great number of bombs and the heavy shellfire, casualties were few. Four came in at 2.00 am and we hear of one man killed. Four men were in the cookhouse at the labour house when a bomb crashed through the roof, killing one instantly and badly wounding the other three. Two other men came in with head wounds from shrapnel.

April 4 and 5, 1917

Raid alarms both nights and shrapnel could be seen far away, but nothing happened. Several flares were dropped from our own planes.

How very backward the spring is this year. The only flowers so far are snowdrops and primroses and the trees show very slight signs of budding, except chestnut and elder.

April 21 1917

Interval since last note has been free from raids. Weather has been very stormy and cold with frequent snow. Last night a heavy cannonade was heard and this morning it is being resumed, apparently at the front. Later we heard that the firing was due to a German raid on Calais and Dover and that two destroyers had been sunk and one damaged.

This evening gunfire suddenly commenced and three German machines could be clearly seen making off. I watched them for some time through glasses until they disappeared in the clouds. Later two injured men were brought in and we heard that five bombs had been dropped though we heard none.

Seventeen sailors were brought here for the night from the minesweeper "Nepaulin. She was sweeping in company with the "Lorna Doone" when the latter sighted a drifting mine and signalled. The mine however disappeared and the "Nepaulin" ran right upon it. Every officer except the captain, who was on the bridge, was lost and 30 altogether are missing. The ship sank in two minutes and all those saved had to swim for their lives. She was one of the Glasgow paddle steamers of which the "Duchess of Montrose" has already been lost.

Old Spanish Houses at Furnes

2

A Visit to the Front

Ernest's natural curiosity and readiness to take risks means that he jumps at the opportunity to take a trip to the frontline near Nieuport, close to the Belgian coast, passing through Furnes. The dark background to this visit is that a German gas attack has recently taken place.

April 23, 1917

A day full of interest. I managed to get on a car going up to Coxyde. We went by the straight, poplar lined main road, running alongside the canal, through Furnes. This is a delightful old town with a remarkable square of old houses dating back to the Spanish occupation of the Netherlands. Many houses were damaged by shellfire. On arrival at Coxyde we found things very busy owing to German attack this morning. After a heavy bombardment (which we heard at Dunkirk) they launched gas and succeeded in taking two lines of trenches at Nieuport. Many French were killed or gassed.

Every car of our convoy S.S.A. 19 was out bringing in wounded and gassed. *[S.S.A., Sections Sanitaires Anglaises, motorised casualty evacuation units, which formed part of the support for the French Army. Three were staffed by members of the F.A.U., each with 22 ambulances and staffed by 56 men.]* I walked out to Oost Dunkuik, a village three miles behind the lines along one of the military roads. The village is very extensively damaged, whole blocks of houses being destroyed. Yet people live there and I saw several women and children in the village. One girl had a gas helmet and I believe everyone has to keep one at hand. This morning the gas cloud penetrated several miles behind the lines, to Furnes, through which we passed. A French lorry driver gave us a lift back, quite spontaneously. The relationship between the French Army and the unit are very cordial.

After dinner I set off on a car to Nieuport Ville. I had a memorable ride. Shell holes were everywhere and nearing the town the road runs behind a continuous canvas screen on wood frames and wire, for at this point it is visible from the German trenches. Through the screen we could see numerous dugouts and shelters occupied by the French reserves. Ruined trenches are visible for the old German front line trench runs through the wood. Little graveyards are everywhere, each with a small wooden cross bearing the name and regiment of the dead soldier. At Coxyde, by the way, in the Zouave Cemetery there, some of the graves had crosses made of soixante quinze shellcases (French 75s).

Devastation at Nieuport (E. Proctor)

We crossed the Yser, a narrow winding stream, by Hell bridge, passing the last inhabited house on the wayside. I have never seen such a scene of desolation and horror as the town presents. No house is untouched and in places bricks, timber, iron, plaster and soil are mixed inextricably in big mounds. Here we were only a few hundred yards from the trenches and had to turn off the road as soon as possible. The dressing station was in the yard of what had been a brewery, in a dugout with heavily bricked and cemented roof, but wounded and gassed men lay all around in the sunshine. I turned aside into a garden, evidently once very pretty. The trees were mutilated and half destroyed by shellfire, but were budding and flowers were coming up. Some of the houses were blackened and scorched by fire, and all were bare and roofless. Guns were firing at intervals from amongst the ruins but generally things in the firing line were quiet.

La Guerre 1914-16
L.C.H. Paris

497. NIEUPORT (Belgique) — L'Église et le Cimetière.
The Church and the Cemetery.

The damaged church at Nieuport

Stretchers were still coming in steadily and we loaded up with four gassed men and set off for Coxyde. Here I left the car and joined another to Camp Champermont where we took in three more gassed men and proceeded to hospital near Coxyde with them. This was full, so I left the car and returned on another to Camp Champermont and at this point succeeded in boarding one bound for Nieuport Bains. The road runs to the sea and at Oost Dunkiurk Bains turns up the coast, past forts and dugouts amongst the dunes. Nieuport Bains is nearly as badly damaged as Nieuport. The road we traversed leads straight as a die for the German trenches and a barricade has been erected half across the road as a screen. One car only is allowed up the road at once. No cases were waiting so the driver and I left the car and went exploring, keeping within the ruined houses for here we were only 400 yards from the German trenches. We crossed the road once at a run—a rapid one!—and walked through a soldier's graveyard, then re-crossed and proceeded through gardens filled high with debris to a dugout occupied by the Unit men when on duty up here. Coming back we travelled underground for a continuous way has been made through the cellars, pitch black and very uneven. We passed the mortuary in which lay 40 dead from the morning's attack, poor souls, and several guard rooms full of French soldiers awaiting their turn to go up. The passage leads direct into the trenches but we did not try to penetrate into these today as the time was not opportune. Coming back we left the passage below and came up to cross the road to look at the church. It was extensively damaged but a large cross hung from the roof intact and the altar was not seriously defaced.

Bits of shells lay about in all directions amongst the ruined houses. I looked out of one house right on the beach. The sea was a lovely sight, a sheet of gold in the brilliant sunshine, but barbed wire ran along the beach and I dare not venture out as the Germans directly command it.

A stroll round Coxyde, full of French troops, and a rather cold run home by La Panne (where the King and Queen of the Belgians live) and Adenkerke, crossing the frontier again. Altogether a memorable day.

**A house at La Panne destroyed by a 75 mm
shell from behind enemy lines**

3

In the Midst of War Life Goes on

Air raids are a normal feature of life for everyone including the civilians. In this period he sees examples of the French civilian population and their efforts to survive in very difficult circumstances. The psychological traumas of the war are glimpsed in some patients described as mentally deranged. The threat of gas attacks is in the background.

April 25, 1917

Wakened at 2.30 am precisely to see star shell burst outside and immediately a terrible naval bombardment opened. Four star shells at once made the night as light as day and the roar of the guns, the shriek and explosions of scores of shells all around and over us and the dense clouds of yellow smoke rolling past made a terrifying experience.

A shell hit the French billet across the road, wounding two men with broken glass but not exploding. I saw it later in the fireplace there. One shell cut the top off a tree immediately outside and a dozen fell within a hundred yards. The hospital had a marvellous escape and we none of us expected to come through the inferno unscathed.

DUNKIRK RAID DETAILS.
PARIS, Saturday.
The *Matin* gives supplemental details of the second bombardment of Dunkirk.
Several German destroyers, favoured by the dark night, bombarded the region of Dunkirk on Wednesday morning at two o'clock. The raid lasted ten minutes, and sirens gave the alarm immediately the first shells were fired.
The fire was rapid and intense, and the town and outlying districts were lit up like day by the enemy's star shells. The fire was of no military importance, and only achieved the killing and wounding of peaceful citizens asleep in bed.
Four persons were killed, and fifteen injured. Between 500 and 600 shells were fired, of which 112 have been picked up.
Seven German destroyers participated in the raid, and it is believed they were afterwards engaged with French torpedo-boats. Trawlers subsequently brought in some wounded men from trawlers which had been sunk.—*Central News.*

There appeared to be no reply from the batteries or ships. After eight or ten minutes of incessant firing it suddenly ceased. Fifteen minutes later a ship fired about six shots, presumably an English monitor. I conjecture it had to steam out of the harbour to fire. Later another outbreak of firing took place further away.

At 6 am I turned out and walked round into Dunkirk. Shell holes were numerous and all around. Two hit the naval hospital, wounding an officer and another hit the French billet at the casino, killing one and wounding three out of five. The unwounded man had crouched in the corner under his mattress and had a wonderful escape.

Several houses were hit, one next door to the sisters' billets. Two or three houses in Dunkirk had been hit and some trees. Shell holes on the glacis of the fortifications were very numerous, but the damage done is wonderfully little considering the amount of explosive wasted on us. *[Glacis—a gently sloping bank running down from the walls of the old town of Dunkirk, part of which was only about 200 yards from the hospital.]*

April 26, 1917

We lost a big Handley-Page plane today. I saw the four go out and we hear it was shot *d*own over the sea. A wounded man we have here was very cleverly picked up from the water by a French seaplane. This man had a bullet in the chest. The rest of the crew tried to swim to the land and were drowned. We *h*ear that the Germans tried a new type of plane today.

April 27-29, 1917

Several raids but not serious ones. Weather delightfully clear and sunny. I am enjoying my work in the garden.

Two of three men wounded at Casino in naval raid have died.

May 2, 1917

We are having lovely weather. I saw German machines being fired at this morning about 6.30 am. A German machine was shot down today by gunfire and fell about half a mile away. The pilot was dead, sitting in his seat, when found, but the observer was missing and is supposed to have jumped.

86 DUNKERQUE. — Le Chantier de France. — LL.

Dunkirk, Shipyard

134 DUNKERQUE. — La Sous-Préfecture et les Bassins Dunkerquois. — LL.

Dunkirk, Police Station and Harbour

May 4, 1917

The usual raid alarms and some firing. Today I went over a large market garden kept by an old Flemish man. It was wonderfully cultivated and screened by hedges of plaited rush. This type of fence is very common here and very effective. It is necessary, too, on such a bleak coast, not only as protection from the cutting wind, but to keep back the constantly drifting sand.

Six or seven bombs had dropped in his garden, he said, and one on his house. These people have much courage to stay on but affection for the land must be very strong in them; it has been won in hard fight against circumstances. It is a remarkable tribute to their powers and industry as gardeners that they can produce such vegetables as asparagus, artichokes, lettuce, spinach, onions, etc. as well as splendid fruit trees, on such land.

The old man presented me with some radishes and invited me to enter his house to have some wine or beer. I felt almost sorry to have to refuse to avail myself of his courtesy.

A new and very large type of seaplane has been overhead today.

May 12, 1917

Again I was invited by a little French hunchback, to enter his garden and a beautiful one it was, too, every conceivable fruit and vegetable being represented, even a vine. He had some fine Hamburg fowls (black and white), some pheasants and some Argentine pheasants and showed us the incubator he used for hatching out the eggs. He was most courteous and pressed us to partake of some wine. The hospitality of these people is very marked. I think it is much more evident here than in the Somme district.

The country has been transformed by the delightful mantle of Spring. Apple and cherry trees are in blossom everywhere and today has been a perfect day, only spoilt by that dull growl of guns at the front

Our new gardens here promise well. Pumpkins, marrows, cucumbers, spinach, beans, peas, radishes and potatoes are all showing up now, but the couch grass with its terrible matted roots is a great trouble to us and makes much labour.

I had my first swim today. The water was quite warm and I enjoyed it thoroughly. The coast is so flat that one can wade out for over half a mile.

May 15, 1917

An Arab patient went mad this morning, broke out of hospital and wounded two people with a bread knife and was finally shot by a French sentry. We are having a good many foreign patients now: Chinese, Egyptians, Greeks, Japanese, etc. Some are firemen on the transports and some are here with labour battalions. We have several cases of beri-beri here among the Chinese.

A big explosion was heard at breakfast time and a lofty column of smoke ascended from Dunkirk. At first it was thought that the Germans were bombarding the town with long range siege guns but later we heard that it was an explosion of hand grenades caused by one being dropped. There are rumours that a long-range bombardment is again threatened.

May 19, 1917

Rumours of naval fight. Heavy firing heard last night. It is high tide and I believe another raid is expected.

May 28, 1917

Bombs were dropped at the labour camp last night and three Egyptians were killed outright and over 20 severely injured. The rest scattered in all directions and at roll call today 400 men were missing. The injured were brought here and it was a busy night for the doctors.

June 2, 1917

Several bombs and some anti-aircraft fire at 4.30 am. Apparently only one enemy machine was engaged in the raid.

We are on French ration bread now, very sour and tough stuff; there are no potatoes and our weekly allowance of sugar is only six ounces. We cannot buy ordinary bread at the shop either.

Bathing is very welcome now, although the jelly fish are beginning to show an unwelcome activity and some of us were stung last Sunday.

Everyone in the hospital has been served out with a gas mask and tonight we had a gas drill. The French mask is a horrible contrivance and nearly asphyxiates the wearer. Gas bombs or gas shells are feared.

EARLY MORNING NAVAL FIGHT OFF DUNKIRK.

German Torpedo Boats Race Away from French Ships.

FRENCH OFFICIAL.

During the night of May 19-20, at about 1 a.m., a patrol of four French torpedo-boats met off Dunkirk a flotilla of German destroyers making for that port.

After a short engagement the enemy flotilla withdrew at full speed towards its base.

Our four torpedo-boats returned to Dunkirk, one of them slightly damaged.—Reuter.

GERMAN OFFICIAL.

AMSTERDAM, Monday.—On the morning of the 20th inst. off the coast of Flanders a short outpost engagement took place between German and French torpedo-boats.

The enemy vessels were repeatedly hit by artillery.

Our vessels returned without loss or damage.—Reuter.

June 3, 1917

The usual raid at 5.00 am.

June 4, 1917

A heavy raid started at 11.00 pm and hostile planes were overhead more or less continuously from then until half past one. Between 100 and 150 bombs are said to have been dropped, and seven, in quick succession, fell close to us. The first bombs were of incendiary character and a great fire was visible across the glacis in Dunkirk. The monitors fired occasionally but there was not a great deal of artillery fire.

June 5, 1917

I was on night duty this evening with a man of the REs, brought in as mentally deranged. He was strange at times during the night but I had no real trouble with him. Air raids started at 11.00 am and lasted to 1.30 am. The gunfire was heavier this time. I marched my man off to the dugout.

A nightingale was singing delightfully at dawn despite an intensely heavy bombardment proceeding, apparently from the sea. Today we hear there has been a naval action.

June 6, 1917

My mentally-afflicted friend became really mad tonight and broke out of his ward. It took six or seven men some time to get him back to bed, where he was tied down securely. He was fairly quiet during the night, but made some fierce threats as to what he would do when he was released. He seems to be under the delusion that he is to be killed.

June 7, 1917

No air raid last night. Today I went by car with my patient and another mental case to Calais. The latter was found to have a knife concealed upon him just before we started. My patient was fairly quiet. We released him to let him put his clothes on. He wrote several letters to his friends bidding them farewell as he was about to die. We conveyed the men to 30 General Hospital and then went down to the seashore and ate our lunch amongst the dunes and had a swim.

June 9, 1917

The gardens of the cottagers around Malo on the edge of the dunes are remarkable. The people have turned a wilderness into a veritable Garden of Eden. Looking from the top of a high sandhill across the level plain towards Bergues one is struck by the thrift and industry of the people, mostly old men and the women folk, left by the war. From the sandy soil they manage by ceaseless industry to produce crops equal to those of the best English gardens. As we looked across the plain, every garden had one or more stooping figures busily engaged on the soil, which reminded me of the painting "The Angelus" by Jean Francois Millet.

**A dugout with the ruins of the padres'
house behind (Arthur Vickery)**

Submarine in the harbour lock at Dunkirk

Staff of St Pol Recreation Hut.
Ellis   Poppleston   Fear
Littleboy   Jackson   Park   Milton

Staff of the St Pol recreation hut

June 10, 1917

I visited the service at the "Pig and Whistle" tonight. Over 50 soldiers present and the service was reverently and attentively followed.

June 11, 1917

The 5th Army is making Dunkirk its headquarters, the staff being at the casino so we can expect activity on this front at last. The Belgians have done absolutely nothing for 2 years or more and we hear the British are taking over the line.

4

Attacked from Air, Land and Sea

Dunkirk was within range of the enormous German canons, which could fire a massive shell a distance of over 20 miles and the impact is described in this section. There is also shelling from the sea and bombing from the air continues with monotonous regularity. On a day off Ernest takes the opportunity to visit the historic towns of Bergues. Being a lover of the open air he jumps at the opportunity to vacate a crowded barrack room for a tent.

June 27, 1917

We were awakened at 10 minutes to 5 this morning by big explosions and a column of smoke could be seen over the glacis. Sirens gave two long blasts (the signal for a long range bombardment) and shots fell regularly at intervals of a few minutes up to 11.30 am. The fourth shot hit and exploded a truck of shells at the seaplane base, causing a good many casualties, and the fifth hit the casino, driving a great gap clean through the building.

Dead and wounded began arriving almost at once, 7 of former and 22 of latter. All were smothered with white powder from ceilings and mortar of walls. 48 shots were counted. I am informed that 10 were killed and 15 wounded at the casino.

Later

Two more have died from wounds. One shell fell in a garden 200 yards from the hospital, making a hole five yards across and nine feet deep. Many others fell quite near but we have not heard what loss of life has been caused among the civilian population.

I helped to prepare the dead for burial, a gruesome task.

June 28, 1917

The dreary sirens awoke us again at 5.00 am, an air raid this time, and some bombs were dropped but on the beach.

Dunkirk Casino (E. Proctor)
HQ of the British 4th Army
Hit by long range bombardment

Bergues, old fortifications

Bergues, view from belfry and belfry below

Bergues, cattle market

July 1, 1917

I travelled out to Bergues today hanging on to the back of a French lorry and came back in a touring car! It is a delightful old town, surrounded by picturesque old walls dating back to the 17th century, now overgrown and in ruins in places, but reinforced at some points by modern defences and forts. The gates are all on the drawbridge plan with portcullis. The big parish church is rather plain and uninteresting but the belfry (in Spanish style) is very picturesque. There is a very ancient abbey too, or rather the tower of it. The gendarmerie is also in Spanish style. Several of the towns in Flanders have these reminders of the Spanish occupation. The country is distinctly more varied than around Dunkirk, trees and windmills, churches and meadows make a pleasant panorama from the walls.

Many houses are in ruins as a result of the bombardment of 1915 (May) when the Germans shelled the whole district including Dunkirk.

Senegalese troops are billeted in the town, fit black men, clad in brownish-yellow uniforms and light blue caps.

July 2, 1917

Two planes came over this afternoon and considerable firing. A piece of shrapnel fell just by three of us who were talking and we needed no second intimation to get under cover! The machines were very clear and the gunfire was fairly accurate, but they went off untouched, pursued by English triplanes.

July 3, 1917

Long-range bombardment alarm at 5.00 pm but though we heard the shots they did not fall near. We heard that six shots were discharged on Bray-dunes.

July 12, 1917

The long-range bombardment siren sounded at 2.30 am just before daybreak and ten minutes afterwards an air raid began. Machines seemed to be flying low and several bombs fell. There was heavy anti-aircraft fire.

Bergues, Rue de la Gare after bombardment in May 1915

Bergues, Place Gambetta after bombardment in May 1915

July 14, 1917

Raid at daybreak. I could hear machines coming before siren sounded. First bomb quite near. Ships outside harbour fired and there was a lively fusillade for a few minutes.

Tonight at 5.30 pm we had a sudden invasion of soldiers badly stung by jelly fish. Some were in an exhausted condition and in great pain. The hospital was already very full—French, British, Jamaican negros, Chinese, Egyptians and naval men and we had to hurriedly improvise a ward.

I was stung on Friday last in the evening twice quite badly and had wretched night, so could sympathise with our patients. The jelly fish are large now, nearly a foot across and the slightest touch from them means a sting. The brutes are floating low, not near the surface as they used to do and it is generally the legs which suffer most.

July 19, 1917

I was on duty tonight with a despatch rider who had come off his motorbike in a smash and had hurt his shoulder and sustained cerebral concussion. He was unconscious but talked constantly of the disaster at Nieuport. He spoke of his friends in the Northamptons, who were wiped out there, and of his own journeys through the sand with despatches. He was very restless, frequently trying to get out of bed to go on duty. After injection of morphia he became more quiet.

July 22, 1917

Two machines were over this morning and there was some firing but I don't think any bombs were dropped. Probably they were out for photographs. Hospital still very full; a lot of Indians (3rd West India Regiment) and some Chinese.

July 25, 1917

I vacated the crowded barrack room with profound relief and became a tent dweller.

July 29, 1917

Heavy gunfire from the sea during the night. The sounds moved up the coastline towards us and then ceased abruptly. Gunfire at the Nieuport and Ypres fronts has been incessant and heavy the last few days.

July 31-August 4, 1917

Tremendous rains almost without cessation. The cannonade has been terrific but the weather must be playing havoc with our offensive.

August 4, 1917

Naval observer-gunner brought in today with shattered right leg. He was in an English plane over the German lines and the machine was caught by a hostile plane from behind. The pilot got as far as the beach and then had to land. The leg has had to be taken off and it is doubtful if the patient will survive.

August 5-16 1917

Big raid by five machines at midday. Three bombs dropped immediately outside the hospital and several men from the adjoining medical stores were hit by flying pieces and came in to be dressed.

42 patients were admitted, mostly men working at the docks and from the motor boat patrol. A gang of Chinese labour troops suffered severely, 19 being hit of whom seven have died or were killed at once. Five English soldiers died and many more were severely hurt.

I had a glimpse of the machines one of which seemed to be a big Gotha plane. *[Gotha—a heavy German bomber, first used by the German air force in 1917 and principally at night.]*

The hospital is very full indeed and new marquees are being put up. Heavy rains nearly every day. One consolation is that grey skies mean fewer air raids.

5

A Month of Incessant Bombardment.

After a period of leave in England from August 18 to September 6, Ernest returned to Dunkirk during a month when it was being attacked from air, land and sea with great ferocity. The History of the F.A.U. draws attention to this month as follows: "None . . . can easily forget the strain and anxiety of September 1917. During that month the town and the environs were under almost incessant bombardment from air, land and sea." Some of the time there was no chance to change into one's nightwear. The onslaught continued heavily to the end of October when Ernest had a near miss.

September 6, 1917

Crossed by S.S. "Onward", four ships crossing together, under destroyer escort, one full of Chinese labourers. Calm sea and a fine though hazy day. Stayed the night at the Hotel de France, Boulogne.

September 7, 1917

Proceeded at 3.45 pm by rail to Dunkirk, arriving 7.15 pm.

During my leave the town has had rough handling from enemy aircraft and last week they were over practically every night. One night there was a long range bombardment in the middle of an air attack. Again the hospital has escaped, although bombs have fallen so close that showers of stones and dirt have fallen on our huts.

A new dugout has been started, after long delay.

September 10, 1917

Without the slightest warning of danger, four bombs crashed down just outside the walls tonight, the first hitting an ammunition lorry and blowing the driver to bits. Another man was severely burnt, as the lorry at once caught fire. Women and children and soldiers just by were killed outright or terribly injured. Eight bodies and a dozen wounded were brought in immediately and it was a grim scene in the wards where the doctors were working by flashlight with bombs falling and a furious artillery fire on all around.

The machines were hovering about for nearly two hours and about an hour after the first attack another bomb fell squarely on the chaplain's house across the road and demolished it. Two padres and a lot of soldiers were in the cellar and were dug out unharmed. The big Rosendael hospital was hit, the maternity ward being blown to bits by a torpedo. A sister and six patients (all women) were killed instantly and nine more wounded.

September 11, 1917

Another night to try the nerves. The alarm sounded this time before the first bomb fell. We heard it hissing as it fell so it was evidently a torpedo. It landed clear of all buildings on the glacis, 200 yards from us and was followed in quick succession by several more. Again the machines hovered about for a considerable time and there was terrific gunfire but the later bombs fell further away.

September 12 1917

The first bomb (or torpedo) last night left a huge pit at least 40 feet across and 12 feet deep. No dugout would stand such missiles as these. We had no patients this time but a house at St Pol was struck by a torpedo and many people in the cellar killed or wounded. It was some hours before the survivors could be dug out. We have transferred 50 patients from hospital today.

Another anxious night tonight. The alarms sounded at 8.45 pm and almost at once we could hear the Gotha planes droning overhead. The sound of the Gotha is very distinctive, a throbbing beat which seems to advance and recede. Gunfire again very heavy but the bombs were further away tonight.

Rosendael hospital

Rosendael railway station

There was a frightful disaster at Rosendael Station where a leave train was standing. The first bomb fell right on a carriage and blew it and several Belgian soldiers to fragments. The second (a torpedo) fell immediately at the side of the train and smashed up another carriage and its occupants, also hitting a small cottage nearby and killing three little children. 25 Belgian soldiers were killed outright and 47 more or less severely injured.

Apparently three machines came over at different times tonight or the same machine hovered about and returned three times.

We hear that two German planes were brought down last night.

September 18, 1917

Wet and stormy. It was delightful to rest without fearing an alarm.

September 22, 1917

Had a pleasant trip to Bergues. Found a nice little cafe and had tea in a back room which contained some delightful old furniture.

September 23, 1917

Five shots were put into Dunkirk this morning by a large naval gun in the German lines. The crack of the explosion was very loud and was followed by a long rattling roar and we saw a big column of smoke from three of the shells. I walked into the town this afternoon and found one had fallen just by the English church wrecking the tram lines; another had struck the side of the clock, narrowly missing some vessels, demolishing the strong stone wall and tearing up a railway line. The rest I did not see. I have heard of no lives being lost and only one woman was injured, a wonderful escape considering the size and power of the shells.

A German two-seater machine is on view in the Place Jean Bart, quite in tact, but its history I do not know.

Dunkirk, Place Jean Bart

Raid alarm just at close of our meeting but nothing happened.

September 24, 1917

We played a footer match to the accompaniment of a chorus of sirens, heralding a land bombardment. One shell fell near the harbour but we heard it not!

For the evening there was the usual programme—bellowings from the "cow" (the familiar name for our chief siren), bombs and gunfire, searchlights and fires, as per usual on raid nights.

St Pol seems to have caught it this time in company with the docks. An important workshop at St Pol Aerodrome, set on fire by bombs, illuminated the whole district, and was completely gutted. Again no lives were lost so far as we can hear. Of course we do not always hear of civilian casualties. The planes droned overhead for a long time and it was after 10.00 pm when things settled down again.

September 25, 1917

Sirens at 11 am and shots in the sky but no sign of the hostile plane. Probably Fritz is after photographs. 12 noon more firing, over 100 shrapnel puffs in the sky, which was cloudless, a pretty but sinister spectacle. I sighted the plane, high up, but I think, from the direction of the throb, that there must have been two at least. A shell nose fell very close to where I stood.

A lovely moonlight night and the firing began at 8.10 pm, with opening chorus from sirens. Planes were quite audible and many bombs were dropped. Seven in particular, in quick succession, made a horrible row. The gunfire was appalling for the monitors used their big guns and I think the smaller warships must have been firing too. Some of the crashes shook the whole district. To add to the terrors of the night, big shells from the German lines began to fall about 8.45 pm and continued at regular intervals right up to 11.00 pm, after the air attack had ceased. All the shells seemed to fall in one direction, the harbour mouth but there was no flash and it was difficult to tell. More than once two shells fell simultaneously, showing that more than one gun was in action.

(Later) September 26, 1917

Have been on a tour of inspection tonight. A torpedo fell on adjoining piece of ground right amongst the huts of the R.E Workshops but failed to explode. An incendiary bomb struck a house a few yards away, penetrated to staircase but also did not ignite. Other bombs fell near us and we had narrower escapes than we thought last night. The nearest bomb is not 50 yards from our boundary.

At the Malo gate, a big shell struck the bank of the canal, just missing the bridge into the town, but did no more than throw the stone block far and wide. Most of the shells fell on the docks. Seven bombs fell all around one important office there. I believe no one was injured by any of them. The shells fell in a large group, chiefly, on a road and railway, leaving large holes but doing little more. One landed in a graving dock but it did not touch a ship on the stocks there. *[Graving dock—a dry dock used for cleaning or repairing ships below the water line.]* A bomb, however, struck the forecastle of the S.S. Polescar (formerly a German ship) killing two of the crew and setting her on fire, but the fire was controlled before serious damage was done.

Another shell hit the S.S. "Levnet", a timber ship, on the water line and left her water logged but she is well above water and can be raised. Considering the shower of bombs and shells and the determined character of the attack, the little material damage and insignificant loss of life are marvellous.

The bombardment alarm has been going several times today but no shells have fallen here. A dull cloudy night tonight, and a quiet one.

Dunkirk, railway station and square

Dunkirk, victory statue

September 27, 1917

A most brilliant night tonight and the sirens were sounding by 7.30 pm. Nothing happened for a long time though there was a good deal of shrapnel in the sky towards Calais, and it looked as if a big attack was taking place there.

Towards 9.30 pm enemy planes began to return from that direction and there was some firing. One machine repeatedly used its machine gun in reply but I think only two bombs were dropped, nearly all the machines passing by seawards. The search lights caught one in their beams three times but lost it again.

September 28, 1917

There was a good deal of cloud tonight but enemy machines were over for some time. One appeared to be lost for we could hear it droning about for some time. Then it suddenly appeared below the clouds and the searchlights caught it up at once and it had to run the gauntlet of a very brisk gunfire but eventually got away.

September 29, 1917

A cloudless day and brilliant night and the attack was very fierce and long sustained. I saw one machine in the searchlight beam for some time but the guns failed to hit it. Incendiary bombs were used and there was one huge fire in Dunkirk and several smaller ones. The fire brigade were hit as they worked at the large fire and six men were killed. A seventh was brought in here later, very badly hit, head and leg and will not last the night.

Ten British officers were leaving a café just as a bomb fell. Two were killed and six wounded.

After the raids had finished here, machines kept passing from Calais, where another attack has been taking place; in fact there has been firing all around tonight, shrapnel and stones have fallen on the hospital and some of the bombs have fallen very near.

September 30, 1917

Great damage was done last night and the main streets are badly knocked about, nearly every shop having suffered more or less.

It is stated that 180-200 bombs were thrown upon the Dunkirk district last night. One of our recreation huts had a narrow escape, a bomb falling exactly a yard from the dugout without penetrating but blowing in all the windows and damaging the woodwork.

Dunkirk, la Place Jean-Bart and the tower

40 dead lie in the mortuary of the French military hospital alone.

A bomb fell near us on the glacis but did no harm.

Raid at 12.30 pm today and some bombs and gunfire. Alarms from 7.45 pm up to midnight and German machine guns repeatedly approached but there was no actual raid. It was a cloudless night again and we were fortunate to escape.

October 1, 1917

We are removing our patients to the two dugouts now as soon as supper is over, and, even so, the sirens were going before we had got well under way tonight. Planes were about for some time before the actual raid took place. Over 200 bombs fell up to midnight and great destruction has again been wrought, especially at the aircraft depot. An important workshop was set on fire and the adjoining buildings had to be blown up to save the rest. Seven R.N.A.S. men hit while engaged on the fire, were brought here later and one or two other casualties. *[R.N.A.S = Royal Naval Air Service.]*

Two big fires were visible from the hospital. One machine got in undetected and dropped its six bombs suddenly. I was in the dispensary reading and sought the floor with great celerity for the bombs were very near.

At midnight, just as another raid was starting, a soldier was brought in mad from shellshock and the first bomb fell as we were struggling to get him out of the car. We had a rare tussle to get him to the dugout. As usual I had the job of looking after him, but a couple of our men volunteered to assist me. At first he was very violent while the raid continued but the doctors injected morphia and hyoscine and he fell asleep later.

It was a weary night for we have had little sleep lately and everyone is tired out. I fear we all dozed during the night at intervals.

October 2, 1917

Machines over at 2 pm and considerable firing. I think I heard some bombs.

This was absolutely the worst night we have had, for numerous bombs fell within a radius of 300 or 400 yards from us and the crashes were horrible. Several times I felt certain the hospital was hit. Stones and shrapnel pattered down persistently and lots of our windows were smashed and plaster knocked down. The outside fence and the walls of the huts are pitted with marks. Four bombs fell in a straight line with the fence, about 60 yards distant.

Another fell squarely on the beach battery and killed four of the gunners, wounded seven and put the guns out of action. There was another big fire in Dunkirk. If this sort of thing continues Dunkirk will be practically destroyed.

Clouds came up about 11.30 pm and although a Gotha could be heard later, that finished a rather unnerving night. Soon after, the rain came pattering down.

October 3, 1917

A rather cloudy windy day. We are working to strengthen our new dugout, for these raids made one doubt even the strongest shelters. Our two dugouts have been crowded the last two nights.

Dugouts and huts for infectious cases at the Queen Alexandra Hospital. (E. Proctor)

Inside a dugout. (E. Proctor)

October 13, 1917

A German machine was over at 9.30 am in a brief spell of sunshine, and had a hot reception. The sky was alive with shrapnel but the machine seemed to treat the firing with indifference. We heard afterwards that it was brought down on the return journey.

October 14, 1917

A clear starlit night and a raid began at 6.45pm but the bombs fell some distance away. The Germans released a parachute light which lit up the country brilliantly. Several Scottish soldiers hit at a rest camp near were brought in about 9.00 pm, one of these dying at once. There was a big fire at a factory, damage being estimated at two million francs. Evidently the machines are no longer dependent upon the moon for light.

At St Pol a detention camp is being constructed for prisoners and I saw several Chinese tied to posts within a barbed wire enclosure. One wonders how this sort of thing will affect our prestige after the war.

October 18, 1917

Bombs fell at Malo Terminus, only missing the 4th Army HQ by a few yards. A corporal mounting a horse outside was killed and a soldier wounded, both being brought to hospital. Another attack seemed to be directed upon the docks and a big fire broke out there, amongst some French cars near Malo Gate. Gunfire seemed much less tonight.

Malo les Bains, Place du Kursaal

Malo les Bains, L'Avenue Gaspard Malo

At 12.30 am (Oct. 19) just as we had got to sleep, a naval attack commenced on the town. The sky was alight with star shells and it was as light as day. The attack commenced suddenly and ended abruptly in ten minutes or a quarter of an hour, and scores of shells were fired. Casualties were mercifully light. Five men were brought in from R.E. billets and hit on the staircase as some 200 men were trooping down, and another five from R.N.A.S. Depot (only just moved from St Pol). One of these died in a few minutes and another who was killed outright was not brought here.

One of our largest monitors, (H.M.S. Terror) was badly holed, by, as I understand, a torpedo and was beached to save her from sinking. Where our destroyers were no one seems to know, but there seemed to be no reply to the enemy fire. It was a dark cloudy night, with a very high tide and I presume the hostile flotilla escaped over the sandbanks.

Later (Oct. 19)

The Terror was successfully towed off at noon today and is now in harbour. The news of the bombing of German towns has not cheered us, as reprisals are bound to take place and Dunkirk is certain to suffer. **October 20, 1917**

Down the dugouts as usual most of the evening. We are having unpleasantly clear nights now and the absence of moon makes no difference to the strenuous Boche. Not so many bombs tonight but a good deal of gunfire. No patients in. A big bomb destroyed seven planes in a hangar at the Aerodrome and although a lot of the workshops have been removed, the Aerodrome is still receiving a lot of attention.

Dunkirk, la Place de la Republique

October 21,

Raid in progress by 6.30 pm until 8 pm, machines coming over every few minutes. One crash shook the place. Two soldiers (Military Police) hit by bomb at Place Republique, a quarter of a mile away. Gunfire very strenuous. Mobile batteries (British) are now being used to assist in defence of town. Plane over this morning, photographing, I suppose.

October 23, 1917

Alert at 6.30 pm despite strong winds and heavy clouds. Gun flashes visible and bombs are reported to have been dropped at Adinkerke but none here.

Sleeping in one's clothes is a pestilent practice but most of us are adopting it in these days.

October 24, 1917

Big gale of wind and rain, and we rested in peace—in pyjamas!

October 25, 1917

A gorgeous moonlight night but a big wind and we did not expect a raid, but sirens sounded at 9.30 pm and a sharp attack followed. A house in Rue Caumartin in Dunkirk was hit by torpedos and over 50 people in the cellar killed or wounded. The machines came back towards us and bombs fell with great crashes near, one only a few yards from Sisters' billets. Malo French hospital was struck but no one was hit.

Malo les Bains, the beach

Malo les Bains, Place du Kursaal.
Hotel Pyl, HQ of the FAU, is the tall building at the rear

October 26, 1917

Brilliant moon. "Cow" went at 6.00 pm before it was dark, but nothing happened. The case of the house struck in Rue Caumartin is tragic as it was a public refuge and the cellar was full. 11 bodies had been recovered at 9.00 pm today and rescue parties were still digging.

We lay down about 10.30 pm and most of us were soundly asleep when the sirens went at 10.40 pm. The stuff dropped seemed appallingly heavy and the crashes were very rapid. The gunners seemed to have lost heart and the firing was strangely spasmodic.

October 27, 1917

Horribly light again tonight and we expected trouble, alarms went at 8.00 pm (probably for planes passing over to England) but there was no raid. Most of us slept in our clothes and were agreeably surprised to wake up next morning and find that the night had been quiet.

October 28, 1917

Dunkirk has been heavily hit by recent raids and the destruction goes steadily on. Ruined houses are everywhere and thousands of people are leaving, and after seeing some of the damage today I am pleased that the civilian population is being reduced. The bombs used are of terrific power and blow a house to splinters. I find that bombs again fell quite near to us on Friday. Seven horses were killed on the horse lines about 300 yards away, and a driver was wounded.

A very badly wounded man brought in tonight from HM Monitor "Eribus"(sister ship to "Terror" torpedoes on Oct. 19) which has been torpedoed outside Dunkirk. Raid alarms were sounding as the stretchers arrived at 7.00 pm. Stretcher cases are being taken down the large dugout at dusk each night now.

Raids came very near tonight. A bomb across the road just outside the Hotel du Nord, shook our dugout considerably. Luckily only two horses were killed, but we lost a good deal more glass.

October 29, 1917

Bangs and crashes from 7.45 pm to midnight. The planes seem to do as they like now.

October 30, 1917

Sirens at 8 pm but nothing happened until 3.00 am following morning (Oct.31st) when a sharp attack took place lasting until nearly daybreak. I had a night on duty with an R.N.A.S. Lieutenant O'Connor who went off his head about 10.00 pm. He had some queer delusions, though rational enough in some respects. His chief complaint was that animals were crawling over him. He insisted on leaving the dugout in the middle of the attack, saying he would rather be killed by shellfire than have little black animals crawling over him. A bomb dropped near and he shot off for shelter, and I was not sorry to follow.

October 31, 1917

I went by car to Calais with Lt. O'Connor and delivered him safely at 30 Gen. Hospital there. Calais has been considerably damaged by bombs, though not so seriously as Dunkirk.

We left at 6.30 pm, moonlight night and very cold. Three miles out of Dunkirk we heard the sirens going and saw shrapnel, so we put back for a couple of miles. Raids were over a very wide area and one flight of enemy machines passed overhead for Calais or Gravelines

We spent four hours, half frozen by the roadside and at 12.30 am as all seemed quiet we rushed for Dunkirk at top speed. Just got to Headquarters, when alarums sounded again and further raid began. I had some supper and finally "dossed down" upon the floor of recreation room there. No sleep last night and two hours tonight have left me somewhat sleepy.

A shell nose tore through the roof of our billet and struck the pillow of the man next to me as he lay in bed.

Dunkirk, the Belfry

6

A Quieter Spell but only Comparatively!

Bombardment continues but with reduced intensity. Ernest is now in charge of both outside work and personnel. In view of the constant threats he is increasing the provision of dugouts. There was a desperate fight to control a fire in the hospital. Some space found for Christmas entertainment.

November 1 and 2, 1917

Two dull and windy nights have given us a chance to make up arrears of sleep for which we are grateful.

November 3, 1917

A damp dull day and a dark night with only one or two breaks in the clouds yet we had a raid at 8.15pm, though not many bombs fell. It appears that even bad weather will soon be no protection.

November 4, 1917

Had a long spell of sunshine and clear wind today beyond Mardyke We unwittingly got into the line of a machine gun practice and had to lie in a hollow with bullets whistling overhead for nearly an hour. When we came out we found that sentries and red flags had been posted all along the coast <u>after</u> we had entered the danger zone.

November 5, 1917

The papers today report an attack on British ships by wirelessly-controlled motor boat. This evidently refers to the attack on the "Erebus" (see Oct. 28). It is a wonderful invention the attack being guided by a plane overhead. The boat has no crew, but is fitted with a steel ram and is filled with high explosive and it travels at enormous speed making it a difficult target to hit.

Mardyk

November 11, 1917

A stormy day with clear intervals. I was up the coast near St.Malo Terminus this afternoon and heavy anti aircraft fire was visible near Zuydcoote but the enemy planes evidently found it too warm and retired.

A raid commenced at 9.00 pm but beyond some gunfire we heard little and were not certain if bombs were dropped or whether the machines were proceeding to Calais or England. I found a dozen pieces of shrapnel and a bomb embedded in the roof of our largest dugout today. Scores of pieces have been picked up in the hospital lately including several shell noses. A short raid from 9.30 to 10.00 pm.

November 13, 1917

We got our new dugout partly finished just in time. I left it at 10 minutes to five and at 10 minutes past five a sharp attack commenced lasting with one short interval up to 7.30 pm! Gunfire was furious and there were some bomb crashes.

Two patients only came along, one hit by a bomb on the beach, and the second man from the town.

November 14, 1917

One dead and four wounded men were admitted to hospital this morning casualties from last night's raid! We heard 30 French soldiers were killed and wounded in a dugout on the docks. Two machines over this morning and considerable firing.

November 15, 1917

A hockey match we were playing today came to an untimely end about 4.00 pm as heavy firing suddenly commenced and the shells were bursting directly overhead. Several men picked up shell cases or fragments which fell near as they ran for the hospital and I heard several whiz down near. We were lucky to get back without mishap. Another outburst of firing occurred ten minutes later and a shower of pieces fell upon the roofs.

November 16-20, 1917

Dull damp days with only rare clear intervals. No raids.

November 20, 1917

The papers announced the D.S.O. to Flying Unit commanders Graham and Fisher, both stationed here in the R.N.A.S. Fisher was in hospital here, with an explosive bullet in the knee and I fear he will lose his leg eventually. He was shot over the German lines but succeeded in bringing back his machine. He went on to Calais from here. The leg was quite phosphorescent and emitted a pale light when he was in the operating theatre. On duty tonight with an old soldier of the Royal Marine Labour Company delirious from broncho-pneumonia. He was very restless and I had a busy night. At 3.45 am I thought he would die at once, but he rallied.

November 21, 1917

My patient died at 4pm today.

December 5, 1917

We had to turn out at 12.15 this morning hurriedly. Horribly frosty night and it was painfully cold. The raid was pretty severe and lasted nearly two hours. At 5.00 am we had a second edition lasting until 6.30 am so that our rest was somewhat brief. Some bombs fell in Malo not far from the Hospital and destroyed two houses. A dugout at the detention hospital at St Pol was demolished and seven patients were brought here.

December 6, 1917

Alarm at 2.30 am and onwards until dawn. Very cold night with sharp frost. I turned in three times and then gave it up in despair and stayed up. Very violent fire at times. First bombs were dropped whilst we were getting out of bed. 10 or 11 French soldiers were killed in a hut at St Pol and several wounded.

At 1.00 pm just as we had started dinner another raid took place but we decided to take no notice and went on with dinner. Further siren chorus at 6.20 pm but nothing happened.

December 10, 1917

I was at Dunkirk when the alarm sounded at 7.30 pm and took refuge in a cellar. A Frenchman, his wife and family of six and another Frenchman's wife and child and a further French couple were there and seemed quite unperturbed by the heavy gunfire. The raid lasted about another hour and we then made our way home as quickly as possible.

December 12, 1917

Alarm at 6.30 pm and gunfire had commenced before we had got our stretchers to the dugout. I should think 3 or 4 planes were over but it was difficult to say owing to the heavy barrage and several of the guns were very near to us.

December 17, 1917

A lost airman created an alarm last night by whizzing low overhead in the darkness. He was showing lights and eventually landed at Coudekerque, but came down heavily and the observer got a crack on the head which caused his admission to hospital. The machine had got hopelessly lost in the darkness after leaving St. Omer.

December 18, 1917

A pretty hot raid tonight and some of the bombs were very close. Another big fire at the seaplane base and two men came in injured by a bomb. Another man, a gunner of the anti-aircraft batteries, was admitted having jammed his finger in the breach of his gun. A bit of shrapnel fell on our roofs.

We had got to bed at last, after a further alarm, when the fire bell rang at 11.45 pm. We turned out to find that the kit store and sickbay next door to our billet were well on fire. The glare was visible for miles, and it was evident that it was too late to save the building so we set to work to save our sleeping quarters and mess room at one end and the dispensary and store at the other. It was a pretty desperate fight but we succeeded in isolating the fire at last and by 1.30 am it was under control. The dispensary twice caught but was eventually saved. Our billet was hurriedly emptied of our kits and bedding, and we had a rare task to find our personal property afterwards from the pile. Help turned up wonderfully—R.N.A.S. and jacktars and all the torpedo boats stood by ready to send fire parties if necessary. Luckily there was no raid while the fire lasted or we should have had a wicked time. It was freezingly cold and the water hung in icicles from the hoses.

AFTER THE FIRE

**After the fire in the hospital kit store
and sickbay. (E. Proctor)**

December 20, 1917

I am having a busy time for I am now in charge of all personnel and outside work. Attended a post-mortem today. I had the grisly experience of thawing the body to get the clothes off.

December 22, 1917

Raid started early at 5.10 pm and some heavy stuff was dropped. A billet at Petite Synthe *[part of Dunkirk]* was hit and several men killed and injured. One man died immediately after admission and another was brought in dead. Seven cases (including the dead man) were admitted. Very clear, with brilliant moonlight. Further alarm at 10.45 pm and I heard a machine pass by out at sea, but nothing happened.

Christmas Day

A snowy, stormy day. Two Lieutenants brought in yesterday, both killed in crashes. One turned out be the brother of one of our V.A D.s and an old member of the unit. I started Xmas Day by getting three bodies into coffins, a cheerful occupation. Concerts afternoon and evening.

Boxing Day

Another busy day in the mortuary, seven bodies being there now. More snow and wind. Our Xmas dinner tonight for nurses and men in the big kitchen, followed by games.

December 27, 1917

A naval scrap between destroyers this morning, but no decisive result. Post-mortem this morning on a young seaman from a mine sweeper, drowned after a Christmas Eve drinking bout.

Christmas card from Queen Alexandra Hospital, 1917

REPORT FOR FORTNIGHT DECEMBER 16TH TO 29TH.

E. W. Pettifer is appointed Administrative Superintendent of the Queen Alexandra Hospital and a Sub-officer of the Unit.

Queen Alexandra Hospital.

I regret to report that an outbreak of fire occurred in Ward G of the Queen Alexandra Hospital on Tuesday, December 18th, 1917. This Ward, built of wood and plaster slabs and roofed with corrugated sheets, is used partly as a kit room and partly as the Nurses' Sick Bay. One of the night orderlies heard crackling at 11.45 p.m. and found the kit room end of the ward ablaze inside. He immediately rang the fire bell and summoned the staff. Efforts were at once made to extinguish the fire by means of the fire-hose, buckets, and extinguishers. The two nurses warded in the sick bay were removed to safety; assistance was summoned from the local fire brigade, the Unit and R.N.A.S. headquarters, and arrangements were made with neighbouring hospitals and our own Headquarters to take the patients in case it became necessary to evacuate the neighbouring wards, and all precautions were taken to ensure the safety of all the patients.

The fire was extinguished shortly before 2 a.m. It is believed to have originated in the disinfecting cabin in the Kit Room, where a formalin lamp was burning. The value of the Ward destroyed, the damage to the corridor and Dispensary, and the loss of stores belonging to the Unit and to members will, it is believed, be fairly well covered by the insurance. Warm thanks are due to the various naval contingents and the local fire brigade who helped so largely to prevent the outbreak assuming much more serious dimensions. The hospital staff worked with admirable energy and efficiency. The damage to the Dispensary has been repaired by the Works Department, and accommodation has been kindly granted to us by the French authorities to use a neighbouring building for the storage of kit pending the rebuilding of the Ward.

The first section of the Dug-out for infectious cases has been completed.

"The Friend" January 11 1918 announcing Ernest's appointment as Administrative Superintendent of the hospital and reporting on the fire

7

The Air War

Evidence of the war in the air as a German plane is brought down after an air fight over Dunkirk. Also a chance visit to the Coudekerque aerodrome where the Handley Page bombers are based. The hospital will shortly move to a site near this air base.

January 5, 1918

The interval since my last entry has been quiet, with dark nights and we have had no raid. A machine was over this morning and there was heavy firing. We heard that it was brought down on the return journey, near Bruges, by an English plane.

January 9, 1918

A rapid turnout at 2.15 am today, and bombs and shrapnel were falling by the time we turned out to fetch patients to the dugouts. The machine appeared to be right overhead when we awoke.

January 19, 1918

A dog which appeared to be mad created some sensation about dusk, and ultimately I had to arm a patient with a rifle and get him to shoot it.

January 20, 1918

It was a cloudy night with a half-moon just visible through the clouds last night and an unlikely night for an air attack, but we had a heavy raid nevertheless. The unfortunate seaplane base caught it again and there was a big fire there. Towards the end of the raid several of us turned out to go to a woman who had injured her leg. We found her in a room full of excited French people. The medical officer bandaged her up by the light of a flash lamp.

January 21, 1918

I am working on a new dugout with the aid of several Cape boys, Kaffirs from South Africa. They work well, but jabber away in Dutch all the time.

New device in aeroplane construction. **A British seaplane** with the " Warren truss-wing bracing " instead of frame-wires.

Newly designed British seaplane

January 22, 1918

Out of bed in a hurry at 11.20 pm last night. The raid was a heavy one, 50 bombs being dropped over a wide area, Malo getting several. The evening was very clear and light, and it was curious that the attack did not take place until the sky was nearly overcast. One machine was brought down in Saturday night's raid.

Got another dugout well towards completion today, our fifth.

January 25, 1918

A spotting plane over at midday and heavy firing. At 6.35 pm raids started and lasted until 9.00 pm with brief intervals. At 10.45 pm a terrific crash startled us and there was a wild rush for dugouts. No one could be certain what it was until the sirens began to give bombardment alarms. Six big shells fell with great explosions. After a brief interval further air raids developed and some of the bombs fell very near. Most of us slept in our clothes after this, but a mist came up at 2.15 am and the rest of the night was quiet.

New dugout (E. Proctor)

January 27, 1917

A damaged German plane, brought down near here on Friday night, was on view in Place Jean Bart today. Two wounded aviators were captured with it. The machine was remarkable for its enormous span of wing. More alarms but no raid, though it was a brilliant cloudless night. The Boches are evidently busy at London and Paris.

January 28, 1918

Spotting plane at noon. It is becoming a regular midday stunt. Heavy firing though the machines never seemed in any danger. Again frequent warnings but no raid.

January 29, 1918

Photo planes over at 11.15 and 11.30 am and a good deal of more or less wild firing. At 9.45 pm seven bombs and about midnight eight bombs. Most of us did not disrobe!

**German Gotha plane brought down on the dunes
near Zuydcoote and displayed in the town square**

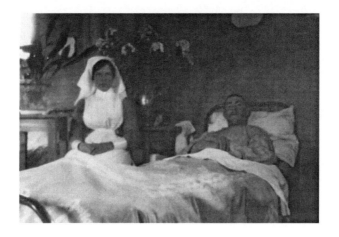

Bed in a French Ward

January 30, 1918

Another Boche over at midday. A drowned R.E., missing since December 25, was brought in from the Docks and we had a pretty horrible job in getting him ready for post-mortem for he was <u>very</u> dead!

February 2, 1918

A plane over at midday today came to grief, being brought down after an air fight over Dunkirk.

February 16, 1918

Four planes over at 11.30 am and heavy firing. Raid alarms most of the evening but we hear no bombs. Later we heard that two fell near the Handley Page hangars at Coudekerque.

February 17, 1918

Visited Coudekerque Aerodrome (R.N.A.S.) and had the pleasure of inspecting the Handley Page bombing machines. We clambered about inside and outside and learnt a good deal. One machine was on its nose buried deep in the ground, the result of a crash last night. No one was hurt though.

More alarms tonight and machines were over, but the raids just now seem singularly ineffective and I assume most of the many machines are busy over England and possibly Calais. Dunkirk as a port has been pretty well paralysed by the frequent raids.

GERMANS' BAD NIGHT.

FOUR RAIDERS SHOT DOWN BY FRENCH ANTI-AIRCRAFT GUNS.

From "The Daily Chronicle" Special Correspondent.

PARIS, Jan. 30.

A Gotha has been brought down by French avions on the beach near Calais, and its occupants taken prisoners. This Gotha was one of a number that raided Calais, dropping bombs in the streets and causing a certain amount of material damage. The number of victims has not yet been announced.

During one night last week the Germans lost nine aeroplanes between the Somme and the North Sea. Several large Hun machines had been sent to bombard Dunkirk, but were caught by French anti-aircraft guns, two being brought down on Belgian territory and two being forced to land in the Dunkirk region. One big machine, which dropped in the flooded Dixmude plain, was a Friedrichshafen Gotha of the latest type, carrying an officer, a sergeant, and two privates, and armed with two machine guns on revolving platforms. It had two 260 h.-p. Benz motors, and its wings measured 85 feet from tip to tip.

When descending the crew threw out all the Gotha's instruments, and after landing tried to burn their machine, but failed owing to the damp. The four Huns were taken prisoner singlehanded by a brave Belgian artilleryman named Joseph Devree, who, pretending to be armed with a revolver, compelled them to raise their hands in sign of surrender.

Sister Nowell, Queen Alexandra Hospital

**Staff of the Queen Alexandra Hospital
Sister Nowell, Dr Farndon
Sister Alexander, Matron**

British Handley Page bomber

8

Moving the Hospital while still under Fire

A new and less vulnerable site for the hospital has been found out of the town, in the grounds of the Chateau de Petite Synthe. Situated among trees it is less visible from the air. It is however near to the Coudekerque Aerodrome where the Handley Page bombers are based. Ernest was responsible for the preparation of the site, putting in the foundations and moving the hutments.

In the middle of the night of 24-25 March a shell exploded in the middle of the Hospital grounds, two men having a miraculous escape. As a result the order was given to move to the new site immediately. The emergency evacuation of all the staff and patients and a large quantity of stores was completed in the course of just two hours. It was clear that the preparation for the move had been accomplished well.

February 18, 1918

At the Chateau to which it is proposed to remove the hospital shortly. Sirens at 6.45 pm and at intervals during the evening but no bombs so far as I know. The alarms are very unsettling though and with all lights out it is impossible to do anything.

February 25, 1918

Many execrations when the "Cow" went at 11.45 pm just as we had all settled down to sleep. We removed patients to dugouts but nothing happened.

February 26, 1918

An American seaplane crashed into the sea just outside the harbour today. The body of the pilot was rescued and brought to the Hospital, but the observer did not come to the surface. This is only the second casualty sustained by the U.S. Naval Air Service so far. The pilot was a finely built boy, a Yale athlete, Ensign Curtis S.

Read. The American officers took two-hour spells on duty outside the mortuary all day and all night. They will find it difficult to maintain this chivalrous custom when they get into real warfare.

Another body came in, a man crushed at the docks.

February 27, 1918

An English officer died today and there are now four bodies in the mortuary. We dressed the body of the American pilot in full uniform today for burial, another curious American custom.

Friends' Ambulance Unit.

The Committee have had under consideration for some time past the necessity of moving the Queen Alexandra Hospital to a more suitable site than that at Malo. It was recently decided to re-establish it at the Château de Petite Synthe, on the south-west of Dunkirk. This removal has been necessitated by the danger of the present site owing to bombs and the inability of the French authorities to send their patients. The official permissions have now been obtained and the authorisations granted. The work of removal has therefore commenced. It is hoped that much of the expense entailed will be met by the authorities concerned.

"The Friend" March 8, 1918

March 1, 1918

Twenty of us left to commence work on the site of the new hospital at "Petite Synthe" Very bleak and stormy with frequent snow squalls.

March 2 to March 19, 1918

Foundations have been put in for three huts and other premises cleared and floored. We have had some assistance from army carpenters and Chinese labourers. Several raid alarms in this period which we could hear clearly, but only one machine over so far.

March 19, 1918

A heavy and prolonged raid tonight. The gunfire is very heavy around here, one battery being only 300 yards away but we appear to be on the fringe of the hostile aeroplanes track so far. Three heavy bombs dropped half a mile away and I saw the flashes. Three more fell in the direction of St. Pol, one an incendiary bomb, distinguished by a red glare as it fell. A terrific bombardment at the front is clearly audible here.

The big canon, which fired from behind German lines

March 20, 1918

Heavy long-range guns have been shelling Bergues and the country between there and Dunkirk today. Another heavy raid from 7.30 pm today, lasting some hours.

Queen Alexandra Hospital.

The third anniversary of the opening of the Hospital which fell on March 2nd found us getting ready to move the Huts to the new site. A party of twelve orderlies with the Administrative Superintendent in charge and a number of the members of the Works Department took up their abode there on March 1st in order to carry out the preliminary work, foundations for the wards, &c. A start was made at taking down the Huts on March 7th, and at the time of writing the whole of Ward H and a portion of Ward Q have actually been transported to the new ground. How rapidly the removal will be performed depends on the somewhat uncertain supply of labour, but certainly events will have moved a good way towards the final transfer before another fortnightly report is due. The anniversary was celebrated by games and a supper on the evening of the 5th. The number of patients treated to date are :—British 6,164; French 1,728; and others 13. Total 7,905. The total number of dental patients treated since October, 1915, is 10,680.

From *The Friend*, March 22, 1918

March 21, 1918

At 5 am a big naval raid commenced, lasting for fully half an hour. The roar of the gunfire was continuous, at first over Dunkirk, but later coming nearer to us. I should think 1300 or 1400 shells must have been fired and we heard the characteristic whine of several passing over here.

The sounds then travelled away and I should conjecture that a naval action followed at once as the firing continued for a long time.

A fuller account of the destroyer action off Dunkirk on Thursday week has shown that eighteen German torpedo craft left Ostend before dawn to bombard Dunkirk. The British destroyers ' Botha ' and ' Morris ' and three French destroyers made for the sound of the guns and intercepted the enemy as he retreated. The ' Morris ' torpedoed a large destroyer. The ' Botha ' rammed and sank another. The French destroyers sank a third. The rest were bombed by a naval air squadron as they fled ; enemy seaplanes coming to the rescue were attacked, and four were destroyed. Finally, one of the enemy ships was torpedoed just off the mole at Ostend. The ' Botha ' was put out of action by a shell through her steam-pipe. The other Allied ships sustained no damage in this spirited little affair.

Press report of the naval battle

(Later) We hear that four destroyers all German were sunk this morning by English and French destroyers and that another was run ashore. An English torpedo boat destroyer was tugged in to Dunkirk harbour badly damaged with 10 wounded and 12 dead on board, all the latter apparently being in one stokehold. More heavy shells on district and the explosions seem to be drawing nearer. Further air raid tonight.

March 22, 1918

Shells have been falling not far away all day. A spotting plane was over at 3.00 pm and, like many of its predecessors, we hear that it was brought down on its return journey. The firing at the front is still very intense and we have just had news of the great German offensive.

Raid alarm but nothing happened.

DUNKIRK'S BOMBARDMENT RECORD,
PARIS, Monday.

Dunkirk holds the record for the number of times a town has been subjected to bombardment of every kind. Up to July 4, 211 air-raid warnings have been given in the town without any projectile having fallen on the town, and 159 warnings have been issued to be followed by bombardment from aircraft.

The town has been shelled 25 times from the earth, four times from the sea, and once from an airship, so that a total of 400 warnings have been issued on different occasions.—Wireless Press.

The severity of Dunkirk's bombardment

March 23, 1918

Exciting times today. Heavy guns have been firing since midday on the town and three shells have fallen within 100 yards of the hospital at Malo.

We had a telephone message tonight to fit up all wards at once as it was possible that the patients and staff would have to be evacuated but eventually it was decided to let matters stand over.

Raid alarms all the evening and some firing but we were too busy to notice much.

March 24, 1918

At 12.30 am I was awakened by telephone and received new that a shell had fallen in the hospital and that all patients and staff were to be evacuated immediately. Shells were still falling. The first bed load of patients arrived a quarter of an hour later and in less than two hours all the patients and staff were here with a large quantity of stores, a remarkable feat. 150 people made a big call upon us at this end but we had everyone bedded down by 4.30 am.

The shell which hit the hospital fell on the site of the hut burnt down in December, and two of our men in a tent had a miraculous

74

escape, the edge of the crater being inside the edge of the tent. One was blown several yards away and struck the carpenters' hut, sustaining some concussion and shell shock but the other was only dazed. A doctor and two orderlies standing three or four yards away were blown down but were also unhurt. Today has been one of strenuous labour for we are in wildest confusion but things have gone admirably despite the heavy and sudden calls made upon us. Luckily the weather is very fine. More shelling at intervals all day and tonight.

March 25, 1918

More shelling of town today. I was at the old hospital and it looks very miserable with material lying everywhere and the huts partly dismantled. The shell hole is a tremendous one and I cannot understand how the men in the hut escaped.

March 26, 1918

Shelling continued; some of the explosions were very near and shook the buildings. I think the shelling gets on one's nerves more than the bombing. Another air raid tonight, and a shell nose fell in the grounds causing showers of shrapnel.

Friends' Ambulance Unit.

REPORT FOR FORTNIGHT MARCH 10TH TO 23RD.

Queen Alexandra Hospital.

Work on the new site has gone ahead considerably during the fortnight, though not as fast as we desired, owing chiefly to the shortage of labour. Three wards have been completed and a fourth is well under way, while a considerable amount of inside work has been carried out in the Chateau. I extend the period of this report by a few hours in order to include the evacuation of the old hospital, which took place at very short notice in the early hours of Sunday (owing to urgent disturbing circumstances). The patients and staff and a considerable amount of equipment were removed by our own ambulances and lorries to the new wards which were rapidly prepared by the staff on the spot. The whole transfer was carried out smoothly and with little or no discomfort to the patients. The staff worked splendidly. The work of transferring the remaining sheds is being expedited as much as possible, and we hope soon to have everything running normally in the new quarters.

The P.M.O. was elected an Hon. Associate of the Order of the Hospital of St. John of Jerusalem in England on February 15th.

The evacuation of the old hospital reported in *The Friend*.

The colossal German shells fired on Dunkirk

9

Fears for Dunkirk as a German Offensive Threatens

A German encircling move if successful could have cut Dunkirk off from the rest of the Allied front, as happened in the Second World War. However by May the situation has stabilised and there was the opportunity for three weeks on leave back in England

March 27, 1918

I went out early and found that one shell had fallen on the French Hospital 600 yards away, and the other in the village. Three large bombs also fell in the village. The school children were gathered round their school house, which had been wrecked by a bomb. We are evidently still well within range of the big shells.

The news of the great German offensive is disquieting for there is a distinct chance of our being cut off unless the advance is checked soon.

Four British West Indian (blacks) were brought in, hit by a large shell while at dinner in their mess room. One was dead on arrival and a second died as soon as he came from the operating theatre.

April 2, 1918

Shelling recommenced about 4.30 pm, about a dozen shells falling. No casualties were brought here.

Chinese coolies are helping in the ward here and I am picking up a few words of Chinese.

April 3, 1918

Awakened at 2.30 am by great crash from a shell. About 13 or 14 fell between 2.30 and 3.45 am. One feels the thud first and this is followed immediately by the report. After that comes the sound of the shells' approach, a large rattling roar and finally we can hear the distant report from the gun, nearly 30 miles away.

Later as I went towards Petite Synthe, I saw one of the craters immediately behind a small cottage on the road to the hospital.

A Handley Page bombing machine came to grief in the mist last night and we saw it embedded in a field. No one was hurt, although it had all its bombs on board when it came down.

Chateau de Petite Synthe

I saw a remarkable mirage today, a great sheet obscuring the fields. A company of infantry marching along a road appeared to be knee deep in water.

April 14, 1918

More shells at 3.00 am today. The Boche is evidently deliberately choosing the night for this cowardly shelling. A gunner was admitted tonight suffering from shell wounds of hand and leg. He was a very big and powerful man and we had to tie him down in bed and drug him. Even so the two men on duty with him all night had a rough time.

April 20, 1918

A big shell at 6 pm at St. Pol, close to where I happened to be and the ground fairly lifted with the explosion. Later from 10 pm onwards, air raids, of which I heard little, being asleep.

**Map showing German advance between February
and June 1918. The evacuation of Dunkirk would
have been triggered if Hazebrouk had fallen.**

Ambulance trains are passing continuously, the only line to the
Ypres front now free being one running past the hospital. Everyone
is under orders to pack emergency kits in case of a hurried retreat,
should the Germans get beyond Hazebrouck.

April 22, 1918

A terrific bombardment at sea tonight in the direction of Ostend.
The whole place shaken by great explosions.

April 23, 1918

News just to hand of the remarkable attacks on Ostend and Zeebrugge. Some wounded are already in from the coastal motor boats.

April 24, 1918

French casualties are coming in very fast, some of them very serious indeed, and we have had several deaths. A number of Belgian refugees have been admitted also: men, women and children, mostly wounded, from Poperinghe. The Barge Hospital is lying close by, also full of refugees.

April 30, 1918

The Germans put a number of big shells into the district this morning, mostly at St. Pol and Mardyke, on our side of Dunkirk.

More severely wounded French are coming in and we are very full. An insane Chinaman admitted tonight.

May 1, 1918

A French soldier, with one leg off, went mad this afternoon. He got out of bed as I was called to the door, and we had a struggle to get him back.

May 6, 1918

Four planes came over tonight before sunset and were vigorously bombarded. We had an excellent view from St. Pol. One appeared to be a Gotha.

May 9, 1918

A rather severe raid about 1.30 am this morning, 40 or 50 bombs being dropped. Two fell on the site of one of our recreation huts at the docks, now just removed to Mardyke. Machines flew very low.

May 15, 1918

An English plane crashed in flames at 12 noon just outside the hospital. I ran round but by the time I arrived only a few fragments remained, and the pilot was lying on the ground, a charred mess. The observer was brought here, badly burnt and seriously injured, but died later.

Entrance to the Chateau

10

A Long Summer of Stalemate

First Sign of a major flu epidemic and some F.A.U. casualties as a result of enemy action. The F.A.U. HQ in Dunkirk at the Hotel Pyl is half demolished by a bomb, killing one of Ernest's former colleagues. More casualties from the Flying Corps. Naval action against the enemy occupied ports of Ostend and Zeebrugge.

June 5, 1918

Left Charing Cross 12.20 pm and crossed from Folkestone by S.S. Stranraer. Lovely day and smooth crossing. Escorted by three destroyers and a couple of other ships.

Stayed night at Hotel de France at Boulogne. Raid alarm at 11 pm but nothing happened. Alarms renewed at midnight just as I had got to bed and a raid started at once, lasting until about 1.30 am, when we got to bed again.

June 6, 1918

At Boulogne I had news of a very severe raid on Dunkirk last night. I am told that it was the worst ever experienced, the aerodrome near us being the objective. I travelled up to Dunkirk by our stores car, a beautiful ride from Boulogne to Calais over the successive ranges of hills, with wide views of the sea and the English coast from the summit.

Calais was raided last night, so the Boche seems to have had a busy night. Arrived at Dunkirk about 7.00 pm. Last night's raid is the one topic and it seems to have been a terrible experience. It was a clear and starlit night and the enemy planes were over tonight by 10.30 pm. The bombing was very violent and rapid. Coudekerque aerodrome again suffered, but no cases came here, the aerodrome having been practically abandoned for the night.

Boulogne-sur-Mer, locks, the Marguet bridge and the post

Boulogne-sur-Mer, sorting the fish

**Doctors' house at Chateau de Petite
Synthe, the new hospital site.**

The moat

The moat

News just to hand that two of our men on Ambulance Convoy number XIV have been killed. Three more men from Ambulance train XVI are in Hospital here, wounded in the big air raid on Etaples. The train suffered a direct hit, the kitchen being destroyed.

June 7, 1918

One bomb fell squarely on the officers' dugout at the old hospital last night. French official reports give the number of bombs for the past two nights as 600.

June 8, 1918

Trouble began before dark tonight, and three enemy machines were clearly seen overhead. There was a burst of firing, and a few desultory shots afterwards, then things settled down again.

June 9, 1918

A short raid tonight. A gasometer was hit and there was a lurid flare. Plenty of shrapnel about us.

June 13, 1918

Firing started without warning at midnight. I heard six bombs but the barrage was very heavy and it was difficult to hear clearly. A big shower of shrapnel rattled on our roofs.

June 14, 1918

Visited Bray Dunes and Ghyvelde. I saw scores of bomb holes near the aerodromes on the way back. The Boche seems to be making many small bombs of the daisy-cutter type, exploding along the surface of the ground.

June 16, 1918

A solitary machine over tonight. Two bombs fell in centre of aerodrome immediately behind us. Royal Engineers are busy protecting our own wards by the erection of earthworks, and are digging trenches for use in emergency.

June 17, 1918

Observer brought in with bullet in abdomen. His Officer Commanding came with him and proved to be Major Robert Lorraine, the famous actor and flyer.

June 26, 1918

About two hours of noise beginning at 1.00 am. The bombs did not seem particularly close but a great many fell on Coudekerque aerodrome again.

June 30, 1918

Heavy air attack last night and another aerodrome caught it badly. Twelve machines and two hangars destroyed.

Had a car ride today to Winckern in Belgium via Furnes (now badly knocked about). Picked up wounded R.A.F.officer and returned via Leysele, Hondschoote and Bergues. Plenty of evidences of last night's raid, which must have covered a wide area.

Great epidemic of influenza, the navy in particular being badly hit. Two destroyers have lost nearly the whole of their crews.

July was a month of intermittent attacks. Ernest finds he is learning to sleep through some of them.

August 7, 1918

The Boche made a vicious attack upon this side of the town last night. Unfortunately, like former days, we had to turn out to receive patients. A "crash" case came in first, a flying officer who had come to grief on the beach, and he was followed by 27 men of the Royal Marine Labour Co., one of them being dead on arrival. A bomb fell between three huts, demolished the lot and damaged five more. Most of the men had stayed in bed instead of going down the dugouts and a number of cases were serious. 100 bombs are officially reported.

Furnes, the old Spanish officers' houses and the theatre

The square at Furnes.

August 9, 1918

Two men of the Royal Air Force in a hut at an aerodrome near by, were killed by a bomb which accidentally fell from an English plane as it ascended. Both brought here.

August 11, 1917

A young Lieutenant brought in tonight horribly mashed up in a "crash" on his first flight in France. He was just an unrecognisable and appalling mess.

August 12, 1918

A very bad raid last night. The Hotel Pyl, our headquarters, was hit and the larger half of it blown down by a bomb, possibly two. Several men fell from the top floor on to the debris without serious injury but two were killed outright. One of the two, F.O. Kitching, had been one of the party in my room for some months and had only just gone to the Pyl. A chimney fell across him and killed him.

Both bodies were brought here. The Adjutant was buried, but was dug out alive after three hours, almost unhurt. Three more came in with slight injuries or shock. The casualty list is mercifully light considering the thoroughness with which the building collapsed.

News is just to hand of another F.A.U. man dead and one wounded by shellfire while driving one of our ambulances further south.

Hotel Pyl, on the left, HQ of the FAU.

Hotel Pyl, half demolished by a bomb.

August 13, 1918

The King visited the hospital today at midday quite unexpectedly. He walked through the wards and inspected the theatre, dental department, bacteriological room etc. and chatted with patients and members of the staff.

August 15, 1918

A couple of hours of noise and anxiety last night. Some very heavy bombs fell, no casualties. We heard that one ammunition dump was exploded at Gravelines.

August 21, 1918

I went by car today, through Calais to St. Inglevert, the new H.Q. of an Aero Squadron. Our patient, who was returning to duty, was a little chap, quite a boy, the pilot of a Handley Page, which came to grief on the beach a few nights ago. The ride beyond Calais was unusually beautiful, through hilly country close to the sea. We had tea on a hill between Cap Gris Nez and Cap Blanc Nez looking across the straits to England. Back via Ghuines, Ardres, Audrieq and Bourbourg.

Friends' Ambulance Unit.

At about 12.30 in the afternoon of Tuesday, August 13th, the King paid a purely surprise visit to the Queen Alexandra Hospital. The Lord Stamfordham, the Lord Cromer, the Hon. Sir Derek Keppel and one of Field Marshal Sir Douglas Haig's Aides-de-Camp were in attendance. In the unavoidable absence of Captain Tatham, who was elsewhere on official duty, His Majesty was received by the Principal Medical Officer (Captain Humphrey Nockolds, D.S.O.) and then made a tour of the hospital, conversing with several of the patients. It is an open secret that His Majesty caused some astonishment among the staff by his obviously intimate knowledge of the details connected both with the administration and with the recent vicissitudes of the hospital. His Majesty was obviously impressed with its orderliness and efficiency and was twice heard to remark, "What a nice place."

During the course of the visit the King was pleased to shake hands with the Matron and several of the Sisters, and requested that Miss Hardy, one of the V.A.D.'s, might be specially presented, presumably for the reason that His Majesty had recently decorated her father with the Victoria Cross.

It is hardly possible to exaggerate the appreciation of the Principal Medical Officer and his staff of the honour of this Royal visit or to express in so many words how much they have been encouraged in their work by His Majesty's kind thought and consideration.

Report of the King's visit to the hospital

The whole countryside was golden with newly-cut corn.

August 22, 1918

Shelling recommenced about midnight last night, and continued for about an hour! I dressed and went out into a corn field behind the hospital. It was a remarkably brilliant moonlight of that hard merciless whiteness which I shall always associate in days to come with many anxious nights out in France.

A great red flash towards Ostend showed when each shot was fired. The pause, 90 seconds, for the crash of the arriving shell, is rather trying.

The sirens were signalling enemy aircraft about several times during the night, and I saw shrapnel sparkling in the sky over Dunkirk up the coast.

August 23, 1918

I had a run on an ambulance this evening on an urgent call from an aerodrome. We got to Pitgam and the wrong aerodrome through a faulty message but finally reached the right place. Only two cases for us a gunshot wound and a shellshock, the rest having been removed to a neighbouring Casualty Clearing Station.

The accident was both curious and destructive. A plane burst into flames just as it was leaving the ground and came down with a rush, the crew just escaped in time, but the blazing plane crashed into two others and fired them. Attempts were made to extinguish the blaze but the ammunition began to explode and the men fortunately scattered.

The bombs on the burning machine exploded and wrecked one line of six cottages, a group of four more, damaged several others and destroyed a hangar. The machine gun bullets set fire to the ruins, so that several large fires were blazing at the same time. Fortunately all the cottagers were out working in the harvest fields close by and there were no civilian casualties.

Raid alarms at 10.00, 11.00 pm and midnight and several heavy gusts of firing.

At 1.00 am today a big bombardment opened from land and sea and numerous star shells illuminated the town. We have no news yet but take it there was some sort of naval attack.

(Later) The official report now states that the bombardment was due to a motor launch attack on the ships lying in Dunkirk Roads, but that no damage was done. The German account claims the sinking of two torpedo craft.

It is remarkable testimony to the efficiency of our Naval Service that though Dunkirk is so few miles from Ostend and Zeebrugge so few Naval attacks take place.

UNDER RAID WRECKAGE.

Thrilling Experience of Members of Friends' Ambulance.

During his recent visit to France the King saw in a hospital in the north four men of the Friends' Ambulance Unit who had been injured when a German aeroplane bombed their headquarters.

Major John Van Schaick, Deputy Commissioner of the American Red Cross for Belgium, in describing the bombing, wrote: "The headquarters of the unit was in the Hotel ——, which was built in two parts. The new part was destroyed. Two bombs fell in the courtyard of the building, blowing out the whole first storey and causing the structure to collapse.

"Two men who were killed were sleeping on the fourth floor. A chimney fell on one and falling beams crushed the other. A worker who was sleeping in the room with one of those who was killed was not injured. Describing his experiences, he said:

"'I had no idea the raid was near us until the plaster started down in sheets, caused by the bomb falling across the street. Then, the two fell which brought us down. The whole room seemed to lurch back toward where the bombs fell, and then went down. My life was saved by my bed shooting across the room.'

"The head of the unit was buried under the débris for three hours. A large oak chest held a beam off his neck. They had to tunnel through the débris to get him out. He was conscious part of the time, and directed the rescuers in their work. He was bruised, but not seriously hurt."

Later report of King's visit

August 25, 1918

Several alarms, some firing last night but I think most of the planes were bound elsewhere. The weather has broken today. Thunderstorms were threatening, a welcome change after cloudless and brilliant nights of this week.

September 4, 1918

A raid alarm last night without result. An observer was brought into the hospital from an aeroplane which landed close by. He was already dead from several bullet wounds received in an air fight.

September 14, 1918

A period of absolute freedom from alarms since my last entry, owing to high winds and frequent rains.

At 3.00 am today a violent explosion awoke us. An ammunition dump about one mile away had blown up. We could hear machine gun ammunition going off for a long time.

September 15, 1918

Three officers brought in today suffering from bullet wounds received in air fights in a big raid on a German aerodrome. A long raid tonight and a big barrage by our guns, but I think Calais caught it worse than we did.

September 17, 1918

A very nasty night last night, lasting until 1.00 am. Three big crashes were very near indeed.

(Later) Three bombs fell last night on the outskirts of the aerodrome adjoining us. 20 bombs fell on Malo and there were two big fires. Our HQ men had a rough night, the R.M.A. workshops close by being burnt out.

September 22, 1918

A longish raid last night. The Bombs seemed to fall in the direction of Burgues. 20 were counted by our men.

September 23, 1918

Another attack and plenty of gunfire and planes but I heard no bombs near. Bergues was badly knocked about last night, a number of civilians being killed.

September 26, 1918

Had a pleasant walk today down the coast near to Loon Plage and back via the village of Mardyck. We tried for tea at the latter place but had no luck. Bread and butter are both only attainable with a card and coal is so scarce that no fires were alight for boiling the water.

Saw two men with flails beating out the seeds of the chicory flowers, a quaintly antiquated method of threshing. Chicory is grown extensively all around this district, the French using far more than we do in their coffee.

September 27, 1918

Long-range guns opened on Dunkirk and district again at 1.15 pm and shells fell regularly every four minutes up to dark. The firing seemed more rapid than usual as if several guns were in action.

11

The Final Push

News filters through of a new attack on the British Front in Belgium. The Hospital is busy with casualties.

September 28, 1918

A few more shells this morning, ceasing about 11.00 am. Our big attack on the Belgian front may have had something to do with this. Our planes were out today despite frequent storms and heavy clouds. Crashes have been frequent, eleven cases, all from the air force, have come in, some suffering from gunshot wounds, and five dead are in the mortuary. Two poor boys came in just at dinner time, one just alive but covered with blood and groaning terribly, and the second one dead.

A big party of machines, caught in a hailstorm, have suffered serious loss, we hear. There has been heavy shelling of Zeebrugge and Ostend by our warships.

September 29, 1918

Heavy storms again all day but our planes have been out. Two more dead in the mortuary.

News is filtering through of the great assault on the western front. A bombardment alarm last night but no shell fell here.

October 1, 1918

More big shells from about 9.00 am, mostly on the docks, and we had two cases in. One a Chinaman was wounded whilst at work there. One shell pitched in a field a few hundred yards from the hospital. Our planes are active again. Pilot and observer in tonight, both badly shot, but they had managed to bring their machine back and alight. Another pilot in, wet through after a crash into the Bourbourg Canal.

GREAT NAVAL ASSAULT ON OSTEND AND ZEEBRUGGE.

BRITISH FORCE LANDED.

STORMING PARTIES OF EAGER VOLUNTEERS FIGHT FOR AN HOUR ON ZEEBRUGGE MOLE.

OLD CRUISERS FILLED WITH CONCRETE SUNK IN CHANNELS.

MOLE WORKS BLOWN UP BY SUBMARINE CHARGED WITH EXPLOSIVES.

The Admiralty issued the following statement yesterday :—

Early this morning a naval raid was made on Ostend and Zeebrugge, which are being used by the enemy as destroyer and submarine bases.

Our forces are returning, and the scanty information so far received is to the effect that the raid met with a reasonable measure of success.

With the exception of covering ships, the force employed consisted of auxiliary vessels, and of six obsolete cruisers.

Five of these cruisers, filled with concrete, were used as block ships, and after being run aground were, in accordance with orders, blown up and abandoned by their crews.

A further communique will be issued when the reports have been received from the ships, which are now returning to their bases.

Report of attack by our warships on Ostende and Zeebrugge

October 2-9, 1918

Nothing doing at all during this period though our planes have been singularly active and several "crash" cases have been admitted. Two brought in yesterday had fallen 5000 feet after collision with another plane, one alive (died later) and one dead. Another pilot was admitted, shot in the arm and back after an air fight, but died shortly after admission.

Had a trip by car into Belgium (Bergue, Rousbrugge, Haringe, Watou and back by Wormhoud). I saw Mount Kemmel and Mont des Chats in the distance.

October 11, 1918

Sudden influx of French malades from French Army engaged on offensive up here. All wards going and very busy.

October 15, 1918

Much to our surprise, shelling started at 8.30 pm. Owing to various "pushes" up here and the reported evacuation of the coast we thought the big guns had been removed. Shells fell very fast in the direction of the docks.

October 19, 1918

Ten or eleven men came in tonight wounded in an explosion caused by a mine near Ostend. They belonged to H.M.S. minesweeper "Plumpton", which sank. Owing to influenza, we are crowded out tonight and were short of men.

October 20, 1918

Influenza very alarming, and hospital is very crowded. We have had many deaths from pneumonia.

November 1, 1918

Nothing of interest since last entry. We have been harder pressed than I ever remember and the mortality has been very serious.

12

Visit to Bruges and the Move to Courtrai.

A one-day visit to Bruges, a town so remarkably unscathed by contrast with all around. The next day a permanent move to Courtrai, passing through Ypres and Menin, revealing the worst of war's brutal devastation. The Convent du Fort in Courtrai will be the base for the rest of the time.

November 2, 1918

I went to Bruges by car, via Furnes, which has been considerably battered since I last saw it and the town is almost deserted with grass growing in the streets. We travelled through Pervyse, held by the Belgians for four years and now in a shapeless heap of ruins.

From that point the road ran through the submerged country which formed no man's land, a weary desolation of rank grass and rushes, mud and ruins. Outposts were reached by duckboards about five feet above the ground and it must have been perilous work relieving the outposts in the darkness.

On the German side the defences had been recently wrecked by a terrible bombardment, the shell holes being thick everywhere. Beyond the road suddenly improved save that all the bridges had gone and from Ghistelle a wonderful avenue vivid with autumn tints led into Bruges.

A big bridge at the entrance to the town was destroyed, but the town gate had not been touched fortunately. We drove through streets gay with flags and emblems of welcome and I was surprised to see the prosperous appearance of the shops. So far as I saw no damage had been done, and I was told that the Germans only left a park of about 20 machine gunners to dispute the entrance of the Belgians.

Nearly all door knobs, knockers and bell pulls had been removed, but there was quite a display of brass wares in the shop windows.

Bruges, Chapelle de St Sang.

Bruges, Porte St Croix

The shop owners told us that they went to bed with the Boche still in possession of the town but awoke to find the Belgian soldiers marching through the streets. The inhabitants had been kept very short of food but otherwise were not actively ill treated.

November 3, 1918

Away at 11.00 am for the new Belgian Civilian Hospital at Courtrai. Route via Bergues, Rousbrugge and Flamentinghe, the latter being badly flattened out. We ate our sandwiches in Ypres Square, amid heaps of grass-covered brick representing the town.

The Cloth Hall could just be distinguished by a few fragments of the walls and tower, but the greater part of the buildings had clean gone.

We passed through the Menin Gate, the entrance to the grave for thousands of British soldiers, and turned to the right, past the desolate cemeteries, on to the battlefields. Hell Corner, Hooge, Gheluvelt, Geluhve, and Menin (the three first merely names on boards now) were the main points in the wilderness of shell hole, ruined trenches and dugouts, tree stumps, graves, ruined tanks, etc. How men lived at all up there on the low ridges passes understanding. The shell holes touched or encroached upon each other for miles and there was no living tree until nearing Menin. This town had been heavily shelled, but not like Ypres. It was curious to find that nearly every roof had gone and all woodwork, and I think the Boche must have made the town a hunting ground for fuel.

Ypres, panorama of the ruins.

Ypres, ruins of the belfry.

We broke down in Swevelghem [between Menin and Courtrai] and Dr Adair and I wandered through the village while we waited and into the cemetery. Here were 56 German graves and amongst them one to an English soldier. The inscription was: Sergeant William Whifford, 18th Regiment, London Corps.

The villages approaching Courtrai had been shelled, but not seriously. The bridges were blown up and a number of houses appeared to have been bombed or shelled.

We found the hospital at the Convent du Fort, a large and fine building, formerly a big boarding school, but latterly a German hospital. The place was in great confusion for the numbers of patients brought in practically overwhelmed the small staff. The reception room was crowded with gassed, wounded, shell-shocked or ill people, and Dr. Adair and I turned to at once amongst the stretchers lying on the floor. The patients were of all ages from babies to old men and women, and the bulk were either gassed or wounded. I have never seen such a mass of misery. Most of the gas cases were horribly burned on face, hands and feet. Nearly 50 dead are in the mortuary and eight died during the night.

Dr Adair, American Red Cross.

Ambulance du Fort from the road.

13

The Great Shadow Lifted

Initially the situation in the Convent du Fort in Courtrai is one of confusion, with the staff struggling to cope with the large number of cases. The last desperate German strike was to use gas. Most cases being treated there are civilians including many gas cases. Then on November 10 the sounds of war are replaced by the sounds of peace. "I knew that at last the Great Shadow had lifted and that peace had come again to a suffering world". But still the casualties come in including children with hand grenade injuries and more gas cases.

November 4, 1918

Had a brief look round the Convent first thing. It is a lovely place, even now when neglected and dirty, and stands in spacious grounds on the banks of the Lys. It has been used for four years as a German hospital and their notices still appear on the walls. The staff comprised 14 Sisters of Charity, eight monks, some voluntary workers from the town, and two doctors and some men of the F.A.U.

Ambulance du Fort from the garden.

All the morning I have been receiving patients and dealing with those who were only out patients. A load of wounded, all hit by shells, came in at 10.00 pm and it was after 11.00 pm when I got to bed. Up at 1.30 am until 4.00 am.

November 5. 1918

Many more deaths. Cases come in steadily all day and the hospital is still very crowded. Dressings most of the day and receiving patients. One old woman was wounded by the last shell, which pitched into her village and her son killed. A man, his son and daughter, were admitted, all wounded by bomb. The same bomb killed the mother and another son. A baby, six weeks old, hit by shell, also brought in.

November 6, 1918

A quiet morning but a wicked afternoon. 21 gassed cases, from old people of 70 to babies a few weeks old, a dreadful sight. Many wounded and sick also. Every bed full

Had a few minutes outside and crossed the Lys by two precarious footbridges thrown over by British in place of the big bridges blown up by the Boche. Two fine old towers behind the hospital, formerly connected by a picturesque stone bridge (destroyed by the enemy) are very conspicuous. I was on night duty in wards from 10.30-12.30 pm and the sights and sounds were heart-rending. All the gassed cases from this morning are already quite blind and some are dead already.

November 7, 1918

Steady work all morning but another influx of gas cases in the afternoon and evening, all from the same town, Iseghem. Several more tiny babies and one old man of 80, and another of 82.

The Boche seems to have thoroughly cleaned up all brass, zinc and steel from the town, and has left the gas, water and electricity supplies all cut off. We are dependent upon old wells for water supply. Even pipes used for pumping out the cesspits have gone, so that for the present it is impossible to empty these.

November 8 and 9, 1918

Busy days with many outpatients and a number of cases for admission. Visited the Beguinage, a famous old place much used by painters. So far as I can gather it is a kind of unofficial convent for wealthy women who wish to retire from the world, without actually entering a convent, and who devote their lives to prayer and charity.

Ten operations on the eighth, several deaths each day. An old woman brought in very ill died suddenly on the floor of the receiving room.

Beguinage from the main gate

Beguinage with Notre Dames behind.

November 10, 1918, THE DAY!!

I was in the messroom when many engine whistles and sirens began to sound about 9.30 pm and going out I heard cheering and saw rockets so I knew that at last the Great Shadow had lifted and that peace had come again to a suffering world.

I went into the town which was thronged with British soldiers and the townspeople. Guns and rockets were firing and the searchlights were ablaze. The brilliant light and shade of Notre Dame with its three big towers, the almost tearful excitement, and the carillon sounding above the multitude of other sounds, I shall not soon forget.

Even peace brought death to one man, for a soldier was brought in dead, his face shattered by a falling rocket stick.

November 11, 1918

Already we feel the relief of peace for few patients have been admitted today. One man came in in a frightful condition from the explosion of a hand grenade with which he was playing—both eyes gone, one hand and part of the other and many wounds all over the body. The operation lasted over 3 hours, but he lived through it.

I fear that many, in fact most of the gassed cases, are doomed for several more have died. At Audenarde I hear that 500 people have perished in their cellars from gas.

November 12, 1918

A review of British Troops took place today in the market place, by Gen. Jacob, commanding the 19th Corps.

Three patients discharged from the hospital this morning after a fortnight here from gas, returned tonight again, gassed in their home at Avelghem, the gas having remained in the room the whole of that time.

November 13-14, 1918

The hospital steadily quietens down, but we still receive casualties, a man with eyes destroyed and hands blown off from grenade explosion, a boy badly burnt in the leg by phosphorous, another burnt in face by explosion of powder, and so on.

Victory review of troops with king Albert and President Poincare in the Square at Furnes

The streets are full of returning refugees strange little processions of those who have been homeless for so long. Here a man pushing a wheelbarrow piled up with all he has in the world, a baby on top, his wife, trudging beside him. There a train of three or four small three wheeler wagons drawn by a couple of oxen or cows, most often it is a small cart laden high with chairs and bedding, and drawn by the entire family.

Endless columns of English transport rumble through the streets on their way to the Rhine, and several sad columns of returning English prisoners have passed through, the men looking spent and worn and clad in the strangest motley of garments.

November 15, 1918

I attended the "Te Deum" at the Cathedral today (St. Alberts Day) a showy and spectacular gathering without spiritual significance. Many English Generals and officers were present, and seats were reserved for the staff of the hospital.

A few sick and wounded struggle in but the bulk of our work is over.

Courtrai, market square and bell tower

November 15-22, 1918

Days of quiet routine. Several cases of accidental injury and wounds from explosions of grenades. Five terribly burnt cases came in on the 21st, as a result of an explosion. It is said that when some coal was taken from a heap and placed on the fire there was a blinding flame and big explosions. Dressings for these cases were a most difficult job, for all the upper parts of the body were burned, back and front.

**Staff at the Ambulance du Fort,
Ernest seated centre**

November 23-29, 1918

Four more cases (all boys) burnt by powder explosion and several more cases.

Visited Tourcoing and Roubaix [*both just south of Courtrai and close to Lille*] prosperous and large towns of northern France.

November 30-December 5, 1918

More casualties. A man who picked up a hand grenade and lost a couple of fingers, a boy who did the same and lost four fingers, and so on.

December 7, 1918

Visited the Mont de Pieli, a curious old building used as a sort of municipal pawn shop, and now crammed with valuable goods of all kinds, furniture, jewellery, pottery, clothing etc., placed here for safety during the German occupation. Curiously the Boche appears not to have entered the place, or he would have had a fine haul.

December 8, 1918

Walked along the Ghent road as far as Harlebeke, the river Lys on the left. Heavy fighting had taken place along this road and there were hundreds of shell holes and a number of graves. The sides of the road were lined with machine-gun emplacements and below, across the river, there was still the little pontoon bridge used by the British in crossing.

December 9, 1918

Walked to Cuerne, along the Lys. Hundreds of shell holes pitted the meadows and the village is badly shattered by German bombardment, the village being held by the British and the main crossing of the Lys being effected here. A gentleman enjoying himself with a gun across the river dropped a bullet in the water, a few yards from me. Unfortunately I could not get across so could not express my views as I should have liked to do.

December 10-24, 1918

Patients slowly decreasing but out-patients coming in greater numbers. There is a considerable amount of skin disease due partly no doubt to the lack of soap and water in the town. The water supply is still cut off, thanks to the Boche.

December 25, 1918

The quietest Christmas Day I have ever spent.

Boxing Day

We reached a total of 50 out-patients this morning, our highest figure. Our total already exceeds 1000. The Belgian Committee gave a big and rather formal tea and concert in our honour.

December 27, 1918

Another grenade accident, a boy with one hand off and an eye destroyed. Fortunately he was struck in an eye, which had already been destroyed and so preserved his sight

December 31, 1918

We spent New Year's Eve in games and dancing with some of the Belgian Red Cross workers and had an excellent time.

A derelict tank

14

So Ends My War

After all the strain and stress Ernest became ill for the first time since joining the unit. He suffered from gastro-enteritis, followed by throat trouble and then a skin rash. Eventually back to Newbury on February 7, 1919.

January 1, 1919

A bad start for the New Year. In bed with a sharp attack of gastro-enteritis, my first spell in bed since joining the unit.

Four bad burns in on night of January 3: a mother, daughter and two sons. The mother was literally burned from head to foot and died alone, the daughter next morning.

January 5, 1919

Amongst the out patients was a boy with a cut finger, very black and dirty. Enquiring elicited the fact that the parents had adopted the old remedy of placing a cobweb on the wound.

The Baggerhof, Courtrai.

**A quaint corner of Courtrai
Twelve almshouses from the C17th
reserved for elderly single ladies.**

January 8, 1919

A Fete with music and dancing was given in our honour by the Belgian lady helpers.

January 9, 1919

First men (Geering, Ward and May) left the hospital. Out-patients going up steadily. The amount of skin disease is astonishing.

January 13, 1919

First batch of patients transferred today, either to their homes or to St. Joseph's Hospice. Most of them were very unwilling to leave, and we were very sorry to lose them.

January 14, 1919

Remainder of patients transferred. The hospital looks very desolate. For the present we are keeping a few of our out-patients.

January 15, 1919

Hospital officially closed and most of our men left for Dunkirk.

January 21-27, 1919

Went to bed with sharp attack of throat trouble. In bed all this time, but throat gradually improving. Up for first time on the 28th January and had short walk, though pretty weak.

January 30, 1919

Had severe urticaria following the numerous injections I had against diphtheria. Whole body swollen and much irritated. Had a wretched night. Dodd, the dispenser, left today. Only five of us remain now, and two of us are sick.

The official number of patients treated in the out patients department is 1737 but we did considerably more.

January 31-February 5, 1919

Days of convalescence. The convent seems very dreary now that all work is over. The day school has already started.

Artic weather, severe frost and much snow.

February 6, 1919

Dr. Manning, Greenwood, Maskell and I left for Dunkirk at 10.00 am. Lovely day of sunshine after heavy fall of snow last night and the country was very beautiful.

Hundreds of Boche prisoners and Chinese labourers at work all along the Ypres-Menin Road clearing the snow. The battlefields were softened and made less horrible by the mantle of snow. We took some photos in Ypres square where more Boche prisoners were at work amongst the ruins.

Had an excellent lunch at La Poufree Café kept by an old lady and her daughter, both of whom had stayed in Poperinghe right through the war. They had had one shell in the back premises, but had not been hurt.

We reached Dunkirk at 2.00 pm and I at once made arrangements at H.Q. to proceed on the morrow. The old hospital looks unspeakably dreary and ruinous now and there is a steady flow of men to England.

February 7, 1919

Up at 5 am—a freezing morning with a wind like a razor edge— left Dunkirk for the last time at 7.00 am and reached Boulogne at 10.30 am. Lunch at Hotel de France, and a final look round Boulogne, and then to the docks. The boat was very late in, and we had to wait three hours in the cutting wind, but got away at 4.00 pm by S.S. Invicta.

A choppy sea and a most unpleasant spray, but the sunset, a deep golden one, was magnificent. A destroyer was silhouetted against the setting sun, all her guns (so it seemed) blazing away at a drifting mine. It was dusk when we reached Folkestone, and most of the passengers were very glad to reach firm land again! Singularly I crossed with W. B. Owen, one of the men with whom I went out a little over three years ago.

Reached London at dusk 8.00 pm. No buses, no cabs, no tubes, so I had to foot it with all my kit to Paddington. I got as far as Reading by 9.15 pm, but could get no train further on so put up at Willison's Hotel for the night.

February 7, 1919

Reached Newbury 11.00 am. So finishes my very small share in the European War after three years and 10 weeks.

APPENDIX

WAR MEDALS

**Citation in French and Flemish from
Albert, King of the Belgians awarding the
1914-1918 Civil Cross to Mr Ernest W.
Pettifer, Administrative Officer.**

War Medals

(Colour photograph on the back cover.)
From the left, two 1914-18 medals,
In the middle, 1939-45 Defence Medal,
Special Constabulary Medal with two long
service bars, (Ernest was Superintendent of
the Doncaster West Riding Specials)
On the right, the Belgian Civil Cross, see
the citation opposite.